WATCH ON THE RHINE

WATCH
ON THE
RHINE

A PLAY IN THREE ACTS BY

LILLIAN
HELLMAN

CLEVELAND

NEW YORK

THE WORLD PUBLISHING COMPANY

Published by THE WORLD PUBLISHING COMPANY

2231 WEST 110TH STREET • CLEVELAND • OHIO

By arrangement with Random House, Inc.

TOWER BOOKS EDITION

FIRST PRINTING JANUARY 1943

SECOND PRINTING APRIL 1943

H W

For

HERMAN SHUMLIN

THANKS AND AFFECTION

The following cast appears in the Warner Bros. motion picture, *Watch on the Rhine:*

Sara Muller	BETTE DAVIS
Kurt Muller	PAUL LUKAS
Marthe de Brancovis	GERALDINE FITZGERALD
Fanny Farrelly	LUCILE WATSON
Anise	BEULAH BONDI
Teck de Brancovis	GEORGE COULOURIS
David Farrelly	DONALD WOODS
Phili von Ramme	HENRY DANIELL
Joshua	DONALD BUKA
Bodo	ERIC ROBERTS
Babette	JANIS WILSON
Mrs. Mellie Sewell	MARY YOUNG
Herr Blecher	KURT KATCH
Dr. Klauber	ERWIN KALSER
Oberdorff	ROBERT O. DAVIS
Sam Chandler	CLYDE FILLMORE
Joseph	FRANK WILSON
Horace	CLARENCE MUSE
Mr. Chabeuf	JEAN DEBRIAC
Penfield	HOWARD HICKMAN
Doc	WILLIAM WASHINGTON
Belle	VIOLET MCDOWELL

A HAL B. WALLIS *Production*

Directed by HERMAN SHUMLIN

SCENE

The scene of the play is the living room of the Farrelly country house, about twenty miles from Washington.

The time is late spring, 1940.

————

Act One: Early on a Wednesday morning.

Act Two: Ten days later.

Act Three: A half hour later.

ACT ONE

SCENE: *The living room of the Farrelly house, about twenty miles from Washington, D. C., on a warm spring morning.*

Center stage are large French doors leading to an elevated open terrace. On the terrace are chairs, tables, a large table for dining. Some of this furniture we can see; most of it is on the left side of the terrace, beyond our sight. Left stage is an arched entrance, leading to the oval reception hall. We can see the main staircase as it goes off to the back of the hall. Right stage is a door leading to a library. The Farrelly house was built in the early nineteenth century. It has space, simplicity, style. The living room is large. Up stage right is a piano; down stage left, a couch; down stage right, a couch and chairs; up stage a few smaller chairs. Four or five generations have furnished this room and they have all been people of taste. There are no styles, no periods; the room has never been refurnished. Each careless aristocrat has thrown into the room what he or she liked as a child, what he or she brought home when grown up. Therefore the furniture is of many periods: the desk is English, the couch is Victorian, some of the pictures are modern, some of the ornaments French. The room has too many things in it: vases, clocks, miniatures, boxes, china animals. On the right wall is a large portrait of a big kind-faced man in an evening suit of 1900. On another wall is a large, very ugly landscape. The room is

3

*crowded. But it is cool and clean and its fabrics and woods
are in soft colors.*

AT RISE: ANISE, *a thin Frenchwoman of about sixty, in a
dark housekeeper's dress, is standing at a table sorting mail.
She takes the mail from a small basket, holds each letter to
the light, reads each postal card, then places them in piles.
On the terrace,* JOSEPH, *a tall, middle-aged Negro butler,
wheels a breakfast wagon. As he appears,* FANNY FARRELLY
*comes in from the hall. She is a handsome woman of about
sixty-three. She has on a fancy, good-looking dressing-gown.
Left and right are the audience's left and right.*

FANNY
(*Stops to watch* ANISE. *Sees* JOSEPH *moving about on
terrace. Calls*)
Joseph! (*To* ANISE) Morning.

ANISE
(*Continues examining mail*)
Good morning, Madame.

JOSEPH
(*Comes to terrace door*)
Yes'm?

FANNY
Everybody down?

JOSEPH
No'm. Nobody. I'll get your tea. (*He returns to breakfast
wagon on terrace.*)

4

FANNY

Mr. David isn't down yet? But he knows he is to meet the train.

JOSEPH

(*Comes in from the terrace with the cup of tea*)

He's got plenty of time, Miss Fanny. The train ain't in till noon.

FANNY

Breakfast is at nine o'clock in this house and will be until the day after I die. Ring the bell.

JOSEPH

It ain't nine yet, Miss Fanny. It's eight-thirty.

FANNY

Well, put the clocks up to nine and ring the bell.

JOSEPH

Mr. David told me not to ring it any more. He says it's got too mean a ring, that bell. It disturbs folks.

FANNY

That's what it was put there for. I like to disturb folks.

JOSEPH

Yes'm.

FANNY

You slept well, Anise. You were asleep before I could dismantle myself.

ANISE

I woke several times during the night.

FANNY

Did you? Then you were careful not to stop snoring. We must finally get around to rearranging your room. (ANISE *hands her three or four letters*) Even when you don't snore, it irritates me. (FANNY *opens a letter, begins to read it. After a minute*) What time is it?

ANISE

It is about eight-thirty. Joseph just told you.

FANNY

I didn't hear him. I'm nervous. Naturally. My mail looks dull. (*Reading the letter*) Jenny always tells you a piece of gossip three times, as if it grew fresher with the telling. Did you put flowers in their rooms?

ANISE

Certainly.

FANNY

David ought to get to the station by eleven-thirty.

ANISE
(*Patiently*)

The train does not draw in until ten minutes past noon.

6

FANNY

But it might come in early. It's been known.

ANISE

Never. Not in the Union Station in Washington, the District of Columbia.

FANNY

(*Irritably*)

But it might. It might. Don't argue with me about everything. What time is it?

ANISE

It's now twenty-seven minutes before nine. It will be impossible to continue telling you the time every three minutes from now until Miss Sara arrives. I think you are having a nervous breakdown. Compose yourself.

FANNY

It's been twenty years. Any mother would be nervous. If your daughter were coming home and you hadn't seen her, and a husband, *and* grandchildren—

ANISE

I do not say that it is wrong to be nervous. I, too, am nervous. I say only that you are.

FANNY

Very well. I heard you. *I* say that I am. (*She goes back to reading her letter. Looks up*) Jenny's still in California. She's

7

lost her lavallière again. Birdie Chase's daughter is still faire l'amouring with that actor. Tawdry, Jenny says it is. An actor. Fashions in sin change. In my day, it was Englishmen. I don't understand infidelity. If you love a man, then why? If you don't love him, then why stay with him? (*Without turning, she points over her head to Joshua Farrelly's portrait*) Thank God, I was in love. I thought about Joshua last night. Three grandchildren. He would have liked that. I hope I will. (*Points to other letters*) Anything in anybody else's mail?

ANISE

Advertisements for Mr. David and legal things. For our Count and Countess, there is nothing but what seems an invitation to a lower-class embassy tea and letters asking for bills to get paid.

FANNY

That's every morning. (*Thoughtfully*) In the six weeks the Balkan nobility have been with us, they seem to have run up a great many bills.

ANISE

Yes. *I* told you that. Then there was a night-letter for Mr. David.

(*A very loud, very unpleasant bell begins to ring.*)

FANNY

(*Through the noise*)

Really? From whom?

8

ANISE

From her. I took it on the telephone, and—

(*Bell drowns out her voice.*)

FANNY

Who is "her"? (*Bell becomes very loud*) Go tell him to stop that noise—

ANISE
(*Goes toward terrace, calling*)

Joseph! Stop that bell. Miss Fanny says to stop it.

JOSEPH
(*Calls*)

Miss Fanny said to start it.

FANNY
(*Shouts out to him*)

I didn't tell you to hang yourself with it.

JOSEPH
(*Appears on terrace*)

I ain't hung. Your breakfast is ready.
(*Disappears.*)

FANNY
(*To* ANISE)

Who is "her"?

ANISE

That Carter woman from Lansing, Michigan.

FANNY

Oh, my. Is she back in Washington again? What did the telegram say?

ANISE

It said the long sickness of her dear Papa had terminated in full recovery.

FANNY

That's too bad.

ANISE

She was returning, and would Mr. David come for dinner a week from Thursday? "Love," it said, "to you and your charming mother." (*To* FANNY) That's you. I think Miss Carter from Lansing, Michigan, was unwise in attending the illness of her Papa.

FANNY

I hope so. Why?

ANISE
(*Shrugs*)

There is much winking of the eyes going on between our Countess and Mr. David.

FANNY
(*Eagerly*)

I know that. Anything new happen?

ANISE

(*Too innocently*)

Happen? I don't know what you mean.

FANNY

You know damn well what I mean.

ANISE

That? Oh, no, I don't think that.

JOSEPH

(*Appears in the door*)

The sausage cakes is shrinking.

FANNY

(*Rises. To* ANISE)

I want everybody down here immediately. Is the car ready? (ANISE *nods*) Did you order a good dinner? (*Shrieks*) David! Oh.

(DAVID FARRELLY, *a pleasant-looking man of thirty-nine, comes in from the entrance hall, almost bumps into* FANNY.)

DAVID

Good morning, everybody.

ANISE

(*To* FANNY)

Everything is excellent. You have been asking the same

questions for a week. You have made the kitchen very nervous.

DAVID
(*To* JOSEPH)
Why did you ring that air-raid alarm again?

JOSEPH
Ain't me, Mr. David. I don't like no noise. Miss Fanny told me.

FANNY
Good morning, David.

DAVID
(*To* JOSEPH)
Tell Fred to leave the car. I'll drive to the station.

JOSEPH
(*Nods*)
Yes, sir.

(*Exits.*)

DAVID
(*To* FANNY, *half amused, half annoyed, as he begins to read his mail*)
Mama, I think we'll fix up the chicken-house for you as a playroom. We'll hang the room with bells and you can go into your second childhood in the proper privacy.

FANNY

I find it very interesting. You sleep soundly, you rise at your usual hour—although your sister, whom you haven't seen in years, is waiting at the station—

DAVID

She is not waiting at the station. (*Laughs*) The train does not come in until ten minutes past twelve.

FANNY

(*Airily*)

It's almost that now.

ANISE

(*Turns to look at her*)

Really, Miss Fanny, contain yourself. It is twenty minutes before nine.

DAVID

And I have *not* slept soundly. And I've been up since six o'clock.

FANNY

The Balkans aren't down yet. Where are they?

DAVID

I don't know.

ANISE

There's nothing in your mail, Mr. David. Only the usual advertisements.

13

DAVID

And for me, that is all that is ever likely to come—here.

ANISE

(*Haughtily, as she starts toward hall*)

I cannot, of course, speak for Miss Fanny. *I* have never opened a letter in my life.

DAVID

I know. You don't have to. For you they fly open.

FANNY

(*Giggles*)

It's true. You're a snooper, Anise. (ANISE *exits.* FANNY *talks as* ANISE *moves out*) I rather admire it. It shows an interest in life. (*She looks up at Joshua's portrait*) You know, I've been lying awake most of the night wondering what Papa would have thought about Sara. He'd have been very pleased, wouldn't he? I always find myself wondering what Joshua would have felt.

DAVID

Yes. But maybe it would be just as well if you didn't expect me to be wondering about it, too. I wasn't married to him, Mama. He was just my father.

FANNY

My. You got up on the wrong side of the bed. (*She moves past him. Points to the mail which he is still opening*) The bills are for our noble guests. Interesting, how many there are every morning. How much longer are they going to be with us?

DAVID

(*Without looking at her*)

I don't know.

FANNY

It's been six weeks. Now that Sara and her family are coming, even this house might be a little crowded— (*He looks up at her. Quickly*) Yes. I know I invited them. I felt sorry for Marthe, and Teck rather amused me. He plays good cribbage, and he tells good jokes. But that's not enough for a lifetime guest. If you've been urging her to stay, I wish you'd stop it. They haven't any money; all right, lend them some—

DAVID

I have been urging them to stay?

FANNY

I'm not so old I don't recognize flirting when I see it.

DAVID

But you're old enough not to be silly.

FANNY

I'm not silly. I'm charming.

(MARTHE DE BRANCOVIS, *an attractive woman of thirty-one or thirty-two, enters.*)

15

MARTHE

Good morning, Fanny. Morning, David.

FANNY

Good morning, Marthe.

DAVID
(*Warmly*)

Good morning.

MARTHE

Fanny, darling, couldn't you persuade yourself to let me have a tray in bed and some cotton for my ears?

DAVID

Certainly not. My father ate breakfast at nine; and whatever my father did . . .

FANNY
(*Carefully, to* DAVID)

There was a night-letter for you from that Carter woman in Lansing, Michigan. She is returning and you are to come to dinner next Thursday. (*As she exits on terrace*) C-A-R-T-E-R. (*Pronounces it carefully*) Lansing, Michigan.

DAVID
(*Laughs*)

I know how to spell Carter, but thank you. (FANNY *exits.* DAVID *looks up at* MARTHE) Do you understand my mother?

MARTHE

Sometimes.

DAVID

Miss Carter was done for your benefit.

MARTHE
(*Smiles*)

That means she has guessed that I would be jealous. And she has guessed right.

DAVID
(*Looks at her*)

Jealous?

MARTHE

I know I've no right to be, but I am. And Fanny knows it.

DAVID
(*Carelessly*)

Don't pay any attention to Mama. She has a sure instinct for the women I like, and she begins to hammer away early. Marthe— (*Goes to decanter on side-table*) I'm going to have a drink. I haven't had a drink before breakfast since the day I took my bar examination. (*Pours himself a drink, gulps it down*) What's it going to be like to stand on a station platform and see your sister after all these years? I'm afraid, I guess.

MARTHE

Why?

17

DAVID

I don't know. Afraid she won't like me— (*Shrugs*) We were very fond of each other, but it's been a long time.

MARTHE

I remember Sara. Mama brought me one day when your father was stationed in Paris. I was about six and Sara was about fifteen and you were—

DAVID

You were a pretty little girl.

MARTHE

Do you really remember me? You never told me before.

FANNY

(*Yelling from the terrace*)
David! Come to breakfast.

DAVID

(*As if he had not been listening*)
You know, I've never met Sara's husband. Mama did. I think the first day Sara met him, in Munich. Mama didn't like the marriage much in those days—and Sara didn't care, and Mama didn't like Sara not caring. Mama cut up about it, bad.

MARTHE

Why?

DAVID

Probably because they didn't let her arrange it. Why does Mama ever act badly? She doesn't remember ten minutes later.

MARTHE

Wasn't Mr. Müller poor?

DAVID

Oh, Mama wouldn't have minded that. If they'd only come home and let her fix their lives for them— (*Smiles*) But Sara didn't want it that way.

MARTHE

You'll have a house full of refugees—us and—

DAVID

Are you and Teck refugees? I'm not sure I know what you're refugees from.

MARTHE

From Europe.

DAVID

From what Europe?

MARTHE

(*Smiles, shrugs*)

I don't know. I don't know myself, really. Just Europe. (*Quickly, comes to him*) Sara will like you. I like you. (*Laughs*) That doesn't make sense, does it?

19

(*On her speech,* TECK DE BRANCOVIS *appears in the hall. He is a good-looking man of about forty-five. She stops quickly.*)

TECK

(*To* MARTHE *and* DAVID)

Good morning.

(*The bell gives an enormous ring.*)

DAVID

(*Goes to terrace*)

Good morning, Teck. For years I've been thinking they were coming for Mama with a net. I'm giving up hope. I may try catching her myself. (*Disappears, calling*) Mama! Stop that noise.

TECK

I wonder if science has a name for women who enjoy noise? (*Goes to table, picks up his mail*) Many mistaken people, Marthe, seem to have given you many charge accounts.

MARTHE

The Countess de Brancovis. That still does it. It would be nice to be able to pay bills again—

TECK

Do not act as if I refused to pay them. I did not sleep well last night. I was worried. We have eighty-seven dollars in American Express checks. (*Pleasantly, looking at her*) That's all we have, Marthe.

MARTHE
(*Shrugs*)

Maybe something will turn up. It's due.

TECK
(*Carefully*)

David? (*Then, as she turns to look at him*) The other relatives will arrive this morning?

MARTHE

Yes.

TECK
(*Points to porch*)

I think Madame Fanny and Mr. David may grow weary of accents and charity guests. Or is the husband of the sister a rich one?

MARTHE

No. He's poor. He had to leave Germany in '33.

TECK

A Jew?

MARTHE

No. I don't think so.

TECK

Why did he have to leave Germany?

MARTHE
(*Still reading*)

Oh, I don't know, Teck. He's an anti-Nazi.

21

TECK

A political?

MARTHE

No, I don't think so. He was an engineer. I don't know.
I don't know much about him.

TECK

Did you sleep well?

MARTHE

Yes. Why not?

TECK

Money does not worry you?

MARTHE

It worries me very much. But I just lie still now and hope.
I'm glad to be here. (*Shrugs*) Maybe something good will
happen. We've come to the end of a road. That's been true
for a long time. Things will have to go one way or the other.
Maybe they'll go well, for a change.

TECK

I have not come to the end of any road.

MARTHE

(*Looks at him*)

No? I admire you.

TECK

I'm going into Washington tonight. Phili has a poker

game every Wednesday evening. He has arranged for me to join it.

MARTHE

(*After a pause*)

Have you been seeing Phili?

TECK

Once or twice. Why not? Phili and I are old friends. He may be useful. I do not want to stay in this country forever.

MARTHE

You can't leave them alone. Your favorite dream, isn't it, Teck? That they will let you play with them again? I don't think they will, and I don't think you should be seeing Phili, or that you should be seen at the Embassy.

TECK

(*Smiles*)

You have political convictions now?

MARTHE

I don't know what I have. I've never liked Nazis, as you know, and you should have had enough of them. They seem to have had enough of you, God knows. It would be just as well to admit they are smarter than you are and let them alone.

TECK

(*Looking at her carefully, after a minute*)

That is interesting.

23

MARTHE

What is interesting?

TECK

I think you are trying to say something to me. What is it?

MARTHE

That you ought not to be at the Embassy, and that it's insane to play cards in a game with Von Seitz with eighty-seven dollars in your pocket. I don't think he'd like your not being able to pay up. Suppose you lose?

TECK

I shall try not to lose.

MARTHE

But if you do lose and can't pay, it will be all over Washington in an hour. (*Points to terrace*) They'll find out about it, and we'll be out of here when they do.

TECK

I think I want to be out of here. I find that I do not like the picture of you and our host.

MARTHE

(*Carefully*)

There is no picture, as you put it, to like or dislike.

TECK

Not yet? I am glad to hear that. (*Comes toward her*

24

slowly) Marthe, you understand that I am not really a fool?
You understand that it is unwise to calculate me that way?

MARTHE

(*Slowly, as if it were an effort*)

Yes, I understand that. And I understand that I am getting tired. Just plain tired. The whole thing's too much for
me. I've always meant to ask you, since you play on so many
sides, why we don't come out any better. I've always wanted
to ask you how it happened. (*Sharply*) I'm tired, see? And
I just want to sit down. Just to sit down in a chair and stay.

TECK

(*Carefully*)

Here?

MARTHE

I don't know. Any place—

TECK

You have thus arranged it with David?

MARTHE

I've arranged nothing.

TECK

But you are trying, eh? (*He comes close to her*) I think
not. I would not like that. Do not make any arrangements,
Marthe. I may not allow you to carry them through. (*Smiles*)

Come to breakfast now. (*He passes her, disappears on the terrace. She stands still and thoughtful. Then she, too, moves to the terrace, disappears.*)

(JOSEPH *appears on the terrace, carrying a tray toward the unseen breakfast table. The stage is empty. After a minute, there are sounds of footsteps in the hall.* SARA MÜLLER *appears in the doorway, comes toward the middle of the room as if expecting to find somebody, stops, looks around, begins to smile. Behind her in the doorway, are three children; behind them,* KURT MÜLLER. *They stand waiting, watching* SARA. SARA *is forty-one or forty-two, a good-looking woman, with a well-bred, serious face. She is very badly dressed. Her dress is too long, her shoes were bought a long time ago and have no relation to the dress, and the belt of her dress has become untied and is hanging down. She looks clean and dowdy. As she looks around the room, her face is gay and surprised. Smiling, without turning, absently, she motions to the children and* KURT. *Slowly, the children come in.* BODO MÜLLER, *a boy of nine, comes first. He is carrying coats. Behind him, carrying two cheap valises, is* JOSHUA MÜLLER, *a boy of fourteen. Behind him is* BABETTE MÜLLER, *a pretty little girl of twelve. They are dressed for a much colder climate. They come forward, look at their mother, then move to a couch. Behind them is* KURT MÜLLER, *a large, powerful, German-looking man of about forty-seven. He is carry-*

ing a shabby valise and a brief-case. He stands watch-ing SARA. JOSHUA *puts down the valises, goes to his father, takes the valise from* KURT, *puts it neatly near his, and puts the brief-case near* KURT. BABETTE *goes to* SARA, *takes a package from her, places it near the valise. Then she turns to* BODO, *takes the coats he is carrying, puts them neatly on top of the valises. After a second,* KURT *sits down. As he does so, we see that his movements are slow and careful, as if they are made with effort.*)

BABETTE
(*Points to a couch near which they are standing. She has a slight accent*)
Is it allowed?

KURT
(*Smiles. He has an accent*)
Yes. It is allowed.

(BABETTE *and* BODO *sit stiffly on the couch.*)

JOSHUA
(*Nervously. He has a slight accent*)
But we did not sound the bell—

SARA
(*Idly, as she wanders around the room, her face excited*)
The door isn't locked. It never was. Never since I can re-member.

BODO

(Softly, puzzled)

The entrance of the home is never locked. So.

KURT

(Looks at him)

You find it curious to believe there are people who live and do not need to watch, eh, Bodo?

BODO

Yes, Papa.

KURT

(Smiles)

You and I.

JOSHUA

(Smiles)

It is strange. But it must be good, I think.

KURT

Yes.

SARA

Sit back. Be comfortable. I—I wonder where Mama and David— (*Delighted, sees portrait of Joshua Farrelly, points to it*) And that was my Papa. That was the famous Joshua Farrelly. (*They all look up at it. She wanders around the room*) My goodness, isn't it a fine room? I'd almost forgotten— (*Picks up a picture from the table*) And this was my grandmother. (*Very nervously*) Shall I go and say we're here?

They'd be having breakfast, I think. Always on the side terrace in nice weather. I don't know. Maybe— (*Picks up another picture*) "To Joshua and Fanny Farrelly. With admiration. Alfonso, May 7, 1910." I had an ermine boa and a pink coat. I was angry because it was too warm in Madrid to wear it.

BODO

Alfons von Spanien? Der hat immer Bilder von sich verschenkt. Ein schlechtes Zeichen für einen Mann.

JOSHUA

Mama told you it is good manners to speak the language of the country you visit. Therefore, speak in English.

BODO

I said he seemed always to give his photograph. I said that is a bad flag on a man. Grow fat on the poor people and give pictures of the face.

(JOSHUA *sits down.*)

SARA

I remember a big party and cakes and a glass of champagne for me. I was ten, I guess— (*Suddenly laughs*) That was when Mama said the first time a king got shot at, he was a romantic, but the fifth time he was a comedian. And when my father gave his lecture in Madrid, he repeated it—right in Madrid. It was a great scandal. You know, Alfonso was always getting shot at or bombed.

BODO

(*Shrugs*)

Certainement.

JOSHUA

Certainement? As-tu perdu la tête?

BABETTE

Speak in English, please.

KURT

(*Without turning*)

You are a terrorist, Bodo?

BODO

(*Slowly*)

No.

JOSHUA

Then since when has it become *natural* to shoot upon people?

BODO

Do not give me lessons. It is neither right or natural to shoot upon people. I know that.

SARA

(*Looks at* BABETTE, *thoughtfully*)

An ermine boa. A boa is a scarf. I should like to have one for you, Babbie. Once, in Prague, I saw a pretty one. I wanted to buy it for you. But we had to pay our rent. (*Laughs*) But I almost bought it.

30

BABETTE

Yes, Mama. Thank you. Tie your sash, Mama.

SARA

(*Thoughtfully*)

Almost twenty years.

BODO

You were born here, Mama?

SARA

Upstairs. And I lived here until I went to live with your father. (*Looks out beyond terrace*) Your Uncle David and I used to have a garden, behind the terrace. I wonder if it's still there. I like a garden. I've always hoped we'd have a house some day and settle down— (*Stops, nervously, turns to stare at* KURT, *who is looking at her*) I am talking so foolish. Sentimental. At my age. Gardens and ermine boas. I haven't wanted anything—

KURT

(*Comes toward her, takes her hand*)

Sara. Stop it. This is a fine room. A fine place to be. Everything is so pleasant and full of comfort. This will be a good piano on which to play again. And it is all so clean. I like that. Now, you shall not be a baby. You must enjoy your house, and not be afraid that you hurt me with it. Yes?

BABETTE

Papa, tie Mama's sash, please.

SARA

(*Shyly smiles at him as he leans down to tie the belt*)
Yes, of course. It's strange, that's all. We've never been in a place like this together—

KURT

That does not mean, and should not mean, that we do not remember how to enjoy what comes our way. We are on a holiday.

JOSHUA

A holiday? But for how long? And what plans afterwards?

KURT

(*Quietly*)
We will have plans when the hour arrives to make them.

(ANISE *appears from the hall. She starts into the room, stops, bewildered. The* MÜLLERS *have not seen her. Then, as* SARA *turns,* ANISE *speaks. As she speaks, the children rise.*)

ANISE

What? What?

SARA

(*Softly*)
Anise. It's me. It's Sara.

ANISE

(*Coming forward slowly*)
What? (*Then as she approaches* SARA, *she begins to run*

toward her) Miss Sara! Miss Sara! (*They reach each other, both laugh happily.* SARA *kisses* ANISE) I would have known you. Yes, I would. I would have known— (*Excited, bewildered, nervous, she looks toward* KURT) How do you do, sir? How do you do? (*Turns toward the children*) How do you do?

JOSHUA

Thank you, Miss Anise. We are in good health.

SARA

(*Very happily*)

You look the same. I think you look the same. Just the way I've always remembered. (*To the others*) This is the Anise I have told you about. She was here before I was born.

ANISE

But how— Did you just come in? What a way to come home! And after all the plans we've made! But you were to come on the twelve o'clock train, and Mr. David was to meet you—

BABETTE

The twelve o'clock train was most expensive. We could not have come with that train. We liked the train we came on. It was most luxurious.

ANISE

(*Very nervously, very rattled*)

But Madame Fanny will have a fit. I will call her— She will not be able to contain herself. She—

33

SARA

(*Softly*)

I wanted a few minutes. I'm nervous about coming home, I guess.

BODO

(*Conversationally*)

You are French, Madame Anise?

ANISE

Yes, I am from the Bas Rhin. (*She looks past* SARA, *and bobs her head idiotically at* KURT) Sara's husband. That's nice. That is nice.

BODO

Yes. Your accent is from the North. That is fine country. We were in hiding there once.

(BABETTE *quickly pokes him.*)

ANISE

Hiding? You— (*Turns nervously to* KURT) But here we stand and talk. You have not had your breakfast, sir!

BABETTE

(*Simply, eagerly*)

It would be nice to have breakfast.

ANISE

Yes, of course— I will go and order it.

34

SARA

(*To the children*)

What would you like for breakfast?

BABETTE

(*Surprised*)

What would we like? Why, Mama, we will have anything
that can be spared. If eggs are not too rare or too expensive—

ANISE

(*Amazed*)

Rare? Why— Oh, I—I must call Miss Fanny now. It
is of a necessity. (*Excited, rushing toward terrace, calling*)
Miss Fanny. Miss Fanny. (*Back to* SARA) Have you forgotten your Mama's nature? She cannot bear not knowing
things. Miss Fanny! What a way to come home! After twenty
years and nobody at the station—

FANNY'S VOICE

Don't yell at me. What is the matter with you?

ANISE

Excitedly, as FANNY *draws near*)

She's here. They're here. Miss Sara. She's here, I tell you.

(FANNY *comes up to her, stares at her, then looks slowly
around until she sees* SARA.)

35

SARA
(*Softly*)

Hello, Mama.

FANNY

(*After a long pause, softly, coming toward her*)
Sara. Sara, darling. You're here. You're really here. (*She reaches her, takes her arms, stares at her, smiles*) Welcome. Welcome. Welcome to your house. (*Slowly*) You're not young, Sara.

SARA
(*Smiles*)

No, Mama. I'm forty-one.

FANNY
(*Softly*)

Forty-one. Of course. (*Presses her arms again*) Oh, Sara, I'm— (*Then quickly*) You look more like Papa now. That's good. The years have helped you. (*Turns to look at* KURT) Welcome to this house, sir.

KURT
(*Warmly*)

Thank you, Madame.

FANNY

(*Turns to look at* SARA *again, nervously pats her arm. Nods, turns again to stare at* KURT. *She is nervous and chatty*)
You are a good-looking man, for a German. I didn't re-

member you that way. I like a good-looking man. I always have.

KURT
(*Smiles*)
I like a good-looking woman. I always have.

FANNY
Good. That's the way it should be.

BODO
(*To* SARA)
Ist das Grossmama?

FANNY
(*Looks down*)
Yes. I am your grandmother. Also, I speak German, so do not talk about me. I speak languages very well. But there is no longer anybody to speak with. Anise has half-forgotten her French, which was always bad; and I have nobody with whom to speak my Italian or German or—Sara, it's very good to have you home. I'm chattering away, I—

JOSHUA
Now you have us, Madame. We speak ignorantly, but fluently, in German, French, Italian, Spanish—

KURT
And boastfully in English.

BODO

There is never a need for boasting. If we are to fight for the good of all men, it is to be accepted that we must be among the most advanced.

ANISE

My God.

FANNY

(*To* SARA)

Are these your *children*? Or are they dressed up midgets?

SARA

(*Laughs*)

These are my children, Mama. This, Babette. (BABETTE *bows*) This, Joshua. (JOSHUA *bows*) This is Bodo. (BODO *bows*.)

FANNY

Joshua was named for Papa. You wrote me. (*Indicates picture of Joshua Farrelly*) You bear a great name, young man.

JOSHUA

(*Smiles, indicates his father*)

My name is Müller.

FANNY

(*Looks at him, laughs*)

Yes. You look a little like your grandfather. (*To* BABETTE) And so do you. You are a nice-looking girl. (*To* BODO) You look like nobody.

38

BODO
(*Proudly*)

I am not beautiful.

FANNY
(*Laughs*)

Well, Sara, well. Three children. You have done well. (*To*
KURT) You, too, sir, of course. Are you quite recovered? Sara
wrote that you were in Spain and—

BODO

Did Mama write that Papa was a great hero? He was
brave, he was calm, he was expert, he was resourceful, he
was—

KURT
(*Laughs*)

My biographer. And as unprejudiced as most of them.

SARA

Where is David? I am so anxious— Has he changed much?
Does he . . .

FANNY
(*To* ANISE)

Don't stand there. Go and get him right away. Go get
David. (*As* ANISE *exits*) He's out having breakfast with the
titled folk. Do you remember Marthe Randolph? I mean, do
you remember Hortie Randolph, her mother, who was my
friend? Can you follow what I'm saying? I'm not speaking
well today.

39

SARA

(*Laughs*)

Of course I rememoer Marthe and Hortie. You and she used to scream at each other.

FANNY

Well, Marthe, her daughter, married Teck de Brancovis. *Count* de Brancovis. He was fancy when she married him. Not so fancy now, I suspect. Although still chic and tired. You know what I mean, the way they are in Europe. Well, they're here.

SARA

What's David like now? I—

FANNY

Like? Like? I don't know. He's a lawyer. You know that. Papa's firm. He's never married. You know that, too—

SARA

Why hasn't he married?

FANNY

Really, I don't know. I don't think he likes his own taste. Which is very discriminating of him. He's had a lot of girls, of course, one more ignorant and silly than the other— (*Goes toward terrace, begins to scream*) And where is he? David! David!

ANISE'S VOICE

He's coming, Miss Fanny. He's coming. Contain yourself.
He was down at the garage getting ready to leave—

FANNY

I don't care where he is. Tell him to come.— David! (*Suddenly points to picture of Joshua*) That's my Joshua. Handsome, eh? We were very much in love. Hard to believe of people nowadays, isn't it?

SARA

Kurt and I love each other.

FANNY

Oh. You do? I daresay. But there are ways and ways of loving.

SARA

How dare you, Mama—

KURT
(*Laughs*)

Ladies, ladies.

SARA
(*Giggles*)

Why, I almost got mad then. You know, I don't think I've been mad since I last saw you.

BODO

My! You and Mama must not get angry. Anger is protest. And so you must direction it to the proper channels and then harness it for the good of other men. That is correct, Papa?

FANNY

(*Peers down at him*)

If you grow up to talk like that, and stay as ugly as you are, you are going to have one of those successful careers on the lecture platform.

(JOSHUA *and* BABETTE *laugh.*)

JOSHUA

Ah. It is a great pleasure to hear Grandma talk with you.

BODO

(*To* FANNY, *tenderly*)

We will not like each other.

(KURT *has wandered to the piano. Standing, he touches the keys in the first bars of a Mozart Rondo.*)

FANNY

You are wrong. I think we are rather alike; if that is so, let us at least remember to admire each other.

(DAVID *comes running in from the entrance hall. At the door he stops, stares at* SARA.)

DAVID
(*To* SARA)

Sara. Darling—

SARA

(*Wheels, goes running toward him. She moves into his
arms. He leans down, kisses her with great affection*)
David. David.

DAVID
(*Softly*)

It's been a long, long time. I got to thinking it would never
happen. (*He leans down, kisses her hair. After a minute,
he smiles, presses her arm.*)

SARA
(*Excited*)

David, I'm excited. Isn't it strange? To be here, to see
each other— But I am forgetting. This is my husband. These
are my children. Babette, Joshua, Bodo.

(*They all three advance, stand in line to shake hands.*)

BODO
(*Shaking hand*)

How do you do, Uncle David?

DAVID

How do you do, Bodo? (DAVID *shakes hands with* JOSHUA)
Boys can shake hands. But so pretty a girl must be kissed.

(*He kisses* BABETTE. *She smiles, very pleased, and crosses to the side of* SARA.)

BABETTE

Thank you. Fix your hairpin, Mama.

(SARA *shoves back a falling hairpin.*)

DAVID
(*Crossing to* KURT)

I'm happy to meet you, sir, and to have you here.

KURT

Thank you. Sara has told me so much from you. You have a devoted sister.

DAVID
(*Very pleased*)

Have I? Still? That's mighty good to hear.

(ANISE *comes in from the library.*)

ANISE

Your breakfast is coming. Shall I wash the children, Miss Sara?

JOSHUA
(*Amazed*)

Wash us? Do people wash each other?

SARA

No, but the washing is a good idea. Go along now, and

hurry. (*All three start for the hall*) And then we'll all have a fine, big breakfast again.

(*The children exit.*)

FANNY

Again? Don't you usually have a good breakfast?

KURT
(*Smiles*)

No, Madame. Only sometimes.

SARA
(*Laughs*)

Oh, we do all right, usually. (*Very happily, very gaily*) Ah, it's good to be here. (*Puts her arm in* DAVID's) We were kids. Now we're all grown up! I've got children, you're a lawyer, and a fine one, I bet—

FANNY

The name of Farrelly on the door didn't, of course, hurt David's career.

DAVID
(*Smiles*)

Sara, you might as well know Mama thinks of me only as a monument to Papa and a not very well-made monument at that. I am not the man Papa was.

SARA

(*To* FANNY, *smiles*)

How do you know he's not?

FANNY

(*Carefully*)

I beg your pardon. That is the second time you have spoken disrespectfully of your father. (SARA *and* DAVID *laugh.* FANNY *turns to* KURT) I hope you will like me.

KURT

I hope so.

SARA

(*Pulls him to the couch, sits down with him*)

Now I want to hear about you— (*Looks at him, laughs*) I'm awfully nervous about seeing you. Are you, about me?

DAVID

Yes. I certainly am.

SARA

(*Looks around*)

I'm like an idiot. I want to see everything right away. The lake, and my old room—and I want to talk and ask questions . . .

KURT

(*Laughs*)

More slow, Sara. It is most difficult to have twenty years in a few minutes.

SARA

Yes, I know, but— Oh, well. Kurt's right. We'll say it all slowly. It's just nice being back. Haven't I fine children?

DAVID

Very fine. You're lucky. I wish I had them.

FANNY

How could you have them? All the women you like are too draughty, if you know what I mean. I'm sure that girl from Lansing, Michigan, would be sterile. Which is as God in his wisdom would have it.

SARA

Oh. So you have a girl?

DAVID

I have no girl. This amuses Mama.

FANNY

He's very attractive to some women. (*To* KURT) Both my children are attractive, whatever else they're not. Don't you think so? (*Points to* DAVID) He's flirting with our Countess now, Sara. You will see for yourself.

DAVID

(*Sharply*)

You are making nervous jokes this morning, Mama. And they're not very good ones.

47

FANNY

(*Gaily*)

I tell the truth. If it turns out to be a joke, all the better.

SARA

(*Affectionately*)

Ah, Mama hasn't changed. And that's good, too.

FANNY

Don't mind me, Sara. I, too, am nervous about seeing you. (*To* KURT) You'll like it here. You are an engineer?

KURT

Yes.

FANNY

Do you remember the day we met in München? The day Sara brought you to lunch? I thought you were rather a clod and that Sara would have a miserable life. I think I was wrong. (*To* DAVID) You see? I always admit when I'm wrong.

DAVID

You are a woman who is noble in all things, at all times.

FANNY

Oh, you're mad at me. (*To* KURT) As I say, you'll like it here. I've already made some plans. The new wing will be for you and Sara. The old turkey-house we'll fix up for the

48

children. A nice, new bathroom, and we'll put in their own kitchen, and Anise will move in with them—

SARA

That's kind of you, Mama. But—but—we won't make any plans for a while— (*Very quietly*) A good, long vacation; God knows Kurt needs it—

FANNY

A vacation? You'll be staying here, of course. You don't have to worry about work— Engineers can always get jobs, David says, and he's already begun to inquire—

KURT

I have not worked as an engineer since many years, Madame.

DAVID

Haven't you? I thought— Didn't you work for Dornier?

KURT

Yes. Before '33.

FANNY

But you have worked in other places. A great many other places, I should say. Every letter of Sara's seemed to have a new postmark.

KURT
(*Smiles*)

We move most often.

DAVID

You gave up engineering?

KURT

I gave it up? (*Smiles*) One could say it that way.

FANNY

What do you do?

SARA

Mama, we—

KURT

It is difficult to explain.

DAVID

(*After a slight pause*)

If you'd rather not.

FANNY

No, I—I'm trying to find out something. (*To* KURT) May I ask it, sir?

KURT

Let me help you, Madame. You wish to know whether not being an engineer buys adequate breakfasts for my family. It does not. I have no wish to make a mystery of what I have been doing; it is only that it is awkward to place neatly. (*Smiles, motions with his hand*) It sounds so big: it is so small. I am an Anti-Fascist. And that does not pay well.

FANNY

Do you mind questions?

SARA

Yes.

KURT

(*Sharply*)

Sara. (*To* FANNY) Perhaps I shall not answer them. But I shall try.

FANNY

Are you a radical?

KURT

You would have to tell me what that word means to you, Madame.

FANNY

(*After a slight pause*)

That is just. Perhaps we all have private definitions. We all are Anti-Fascists, for example—

SARA

Yes. But Kurt works at it.

FANNY

What kind of work?

KURT

Any kind. Anywhere.

FANNY

(*Sharply*)

I will stop asking questions.

51

SARA

(*Very sharply*)

That would be sensible, Mama.

DAVID

Darling, don't be angry. We've been worried about you, naturally. We knew so little, except that you were having a bad time.

SARA

I didn't have a bad time. We never—

KURT

Do not lie for me, Sara.

SARA

I'm not lying. I didn't have a bad time, the way they mean. I—

FANNY

(*Slowly*)

You had a bad time just trying to live, didn't you? That's obvious, Sara, and foolish to pretend it isn't. Why wouldn't you take money from us? What kind of nonsense—

SARA

(*Slowly*)

We've lived the way we wanted to live. I don't know the language of rooms like this any more. And I don't want to learn it again.

KURT

Do not bristle about it.

SARA

I'm not bristling. (*To* FANNY) I married because I fell in love. You can understand that.

FANNY
(*Slowly*)

Yes.

SARA

For almost twelve years, Kurt went to work every morning and came home every night, and we lived modestly, and happily— (*Sharply*) As happily as people could in a starved Germany that was going to pieces—

KURT

Sara, please. You're angry. I do not like it that way. I will try to find a way to tell you with quickness. Yes. (SARA *turns, looks at him, starts to speak, stops*) I was born in a town called Fürth. (*Pauses. Looks up, smiles*) There is a holiday in my town. We call it Kirchweih. It was a gay holiday with games and music and a hot white sausage to eat with the wine. I grow up, I move away—to school, to work— but always I come back for Kirchweih. It is for me, the great day of the year. (*Slowly*) But after the war, that day begins to change. The sausage is made from bad stuff, the peasants come in without shoes, the children are too sick— (*Carefully*)

53

It is bad for my people, those years, but always I have hope. In the festival of August, 1931, more than a year before the storm, I give up that hope. On that day, I see twenty-seven men murdered in a Nazi street fight. I cannot stay by now and watch. My time has come to move. I say with Luther, "Here I stand. I can do nothing else. God help me. Amen."

SARA

It doesn't pay well to fight for what we believe in. But I wanted it the way Kurt wanted it. (*Shrugs*) They don't like us in Europe; I guess they never did. So Kurt brought us home. You've always said you wanted us. If you don't, I will understand.

DAVID

Darling, of course we want you—

FANNY

(*Rises*)

I am old. And made of dry cork. And bad-mannered. Please forgive me.

SARA

(*Goes quickly to* FANNY)

Shut up, Mama. We're all acting like fools. I'm glad to be home. That's all I know. So damned glad.

DAVID

And we're damned glad to have you. Come on. Let's walk to the lake. We've made it bigger and planted the island with blackberries—

(She smiles and goes to him. Together they move out the hall entrance.)

FANNY

(After a silence)

They've always liked each other. We're going to have Zwetschgen-Knoedel for dinner. You like them?

KURT

Indeed.

FANNY

I hope you like decent food.

KURT

I do.

FANNY

That's a good sign in a man.

MARTHE

(Coming in from the terrace. Stops in the doorway)

Oh, I'm sorry, Fanny. We were waiting. I didn't want to interrupt the family reunion. I—

FANNY

This is my son-in-law, Herr Müller. The Countess de Brancovis.

KURT AND MARTHE

(Together)

How do you do?

MARTHE

And how is Sara, Herr Müller? I haven't seen her since I was a little girl. She probably doesn't remember me at all. (TECK *comes in from the hall. She turns*) This is my husband, Herr Müller.

KURT

How do you do?

TECK

How do you do, sir? (KURT *bows. They shake hands*) Would it be impertinent for one European to make welcome another?

KURT

(*Smiles*)

I do not think so. It would be friendly.

BODO

(*Appears at the hall door*)

Papa— (*Sees* TECK *and* MARTHE, *bows*) Oh, good morning. Miss Anise says you are the Count and Countess. Once before we met a Count and Countess. They had a small room bordering on ours in Copenhagen. They were more older than you, and more poor. We shared with them our newspaper.

MARTHE

(*Laughs*)

It wasn't us, but it might have been. What's your name?

TECK

(*Laughs*)

We hope you will be as kind to us.

BODO

My name is Bodo. It's a strange name. No? (*To* KURT)
Papa, this is the house of great wonders. Each has his bed,
each has his bathroom. The arrangement of it, that is splen-
dorous.

FANNY

(*Laughs*)

You are a fancy talker, Bodo.

KURT

Oh, yes. In many languages.

BODO

(*To* FANNY)

Please to correct me when I am wrong. Papa, the plumbing
is such as you have never seen. Each implement is placed on
the floor, and all are simultaneous in the same room. You
will therefore see that being placed most solidly on the floor
allows of no rats, rodents or crawlers, and is most sanitary.
(*To the others*) Papa will be most interested. He likes to
know how each thing of everything is put together. And he
is so fond of being clean—

KURT

(*Laughs. To* FANNY)

I am a hero to my children. It bores everybody but me.

TECK

It is most interesting, Herr Müller. I thought I had a good ear for the accents of your country. But yours is most difficult to place. It is Bayrisch? Or is it—

BODO

That's because Papa has worked in so many—

KURT

(*Quickly*)

German accents are the most difficult to identify. I, myself, when I try, am usually incorrect. It would be particularly difficult with me because I speak other languages. Yours would be Roumanian?

MARTHE

(*Laughs*)

My God, is it that bad?

KURT

(*Smiles*)

I am showing off. I know the Count de Brancovis is Roumanian.

58

TECK
(Heartily)
So? We have met before? I thought so, but I cannot remember—

KURT
No, sir. We have not met before. I read your name in the newspapers.

TECK
(To KURT*)*
Strange. I was sure I had met you. I was in the Paris Legation for many years, and I thought perhaps—

KURT
Oh, no. If it is possible to believe, I am the exile who is not famous. *(To* FANNY*)* I have been thinking with pleasure, Madame Fanny, of breakfast on your porch. *(He points to the picture of Joshua Farrelly)* Your husband once wrote: "I am getting older now and Europe seems far away. Fanny and I will have an early breakfast on the porch and then I shall drive the bays into Washington." *(Remembering)* And then he goes on: "Henry Adams tells me he has been reading Karl Marx. I shall have to tell him my father made me read Marx many years ago and that, since he proposes to exhibit himself to impress me, will spoil Henry's Sunday."

FANNY
(Laughs, delighted. Takes KURT'S *arm)*
And so it did. I had forgotten that. I am pleased with you.

I shall come and serve your food myself. I had forgotten
Joshua ever wrote it.

> (*They start out of the terrace doors together, followed
> by* BODO.)

KURT
> (*As they disappear*)

I try to impress you. I learned it last night.

> (FANNY *laughs. They disappear.*)

TECK
> (*Smiles*)

He is a clever man. A quotation from Joshua Farrelly
is a sure road to Fanny's heart. Where did you say Herr
Müller was from?

MARTHE

Germany.

TECK

I know that. (*Goes to a valise. He leans over, stares at it,
looks at the labels, pushes the lock. The lock opens; he closes
it. Then he turns and, as he speaks, picks up the brief-case*)
What part of Germany?

MARTHE

I don't know. And I never knew you were an expert on
accents.

TECK

I never knew it either. Are you driving into Washington with David this morning?

MARTHE

I was going to. But he may not be going to the office, now that Sara's here. I was to have lunch with Sally Tyne. (TECK *puts down the brief-case*) What are you doing?

TECK

Wondering why luggage is unlocked and a shabby brief-case is so carefully locked.

MARTHE

You're very curious about Mr. Müller.

TECK

Yes. And I do not know why. Something far away . . . I am curious about a daughter of the Farrellys' who marries a German who has bullet scars on his face and broken bones in his hands.

MARTHE
(*Sharply*)

Has he? There are many of them now, I guess.

TECK

So there are. But this one is in this house. (*He goes to the bell cord, pulls it. She watches him nervously.*)

MARTHE

Is it—is he any business of yours?

TECK

What is my business? Anything might be my business now.

MARTHE

Yes—unfortunately. You might inquire from your friend Von Seitz. They always know their nationals.

TECK

(*Pleasantly, ignoring the sharpness with which she has spoken*)

Oh, yes, I will do that, of course. But I do not like to ask questions without knowing the value of the answers.

MARTHE

Teck. This man is a little German Sara married years ago. I remember Mama talking about it. He was nothing then and he isn't now. They've had a tough enough time already without—

TECK

Have you— Have you been sleeping with David?

MARTHE

(*Stops, stares at him, then simply*)

No. I have not been. And that hasn't been your business for a good many years now.

TECK

You like him?

MARTHE

(*Nervously*)

What's this for, Teck?

TECK

Answer me, please.

MARTHE

I— (*She stops.*)

TECK

Yes? Answer me.

MARTHE

I do like him.

TECK

What does he feel about you?

MARTHE

I don't know.

TECK

But you are trying to find out. You have made any plans
with him?

MARTHE

Of course not. I—

TECK

You will try to make him have plans. I have recognized it.
Well, we have been together a long— (JOSEPH *enters*. TECK

stops) Joseph, Miss Fanny wishes you to take the baggage upstairs.

JOSEPH

Yes, sir. I was going to. (*He begins to pick up the baggage.* MARTHE *has turned sharply and is staring at* TECK. *Then she rises, watches* JOSEPH *pick up the baggage, turns again to look at* TECK.)

TECK

As I was saying. It is perhaps best that we had this talk.

MARTHE

(*She stops, waits for* JOSEPH *to move off. He exits, carrying the valises*)
Why did you do that? Why did you tell Joseph that Fanny wanted him to take the baggage upstairs?

TECK

Obviously it is more comfortable to look at baggage behind closed doors.

MARTHE

(*Very sharply*)
What kind of silliness is this now? Leave these people alone— (*As he starts to exit*) I won't let you—

TECK

What? (*As he moves again, she comes after him.*)

MARTHE

I said I won't let you. You are not—

TECK

How many times have you seen me angry? (MARTHE *looks up, startled*) You will not wish to see another. Run along now and have lunch with something you call Sally Tyne. But do not make plans with David. You will not be able to carry them out. You will go with me, when I am ready to go. You understand. (*He exits during his speech. The last words come as he goes through the door, and as the curtain falls.*)

ACT TWO

ACT TWO

SCENE: *The same as Act One, about ten days later. During the act it will begin to grow dark; but the evening is warm and the terrace doors are open.*

AT RISE: SARA *is sitting on the couch, crocheting.* FANNY *and* TECK *are sitting at a small table playing cribbage.* BODO *is sitting near them, at a large table, working on a heating pad. The cord is torn from the bag, the bag is ripped open.* ANISE *sits next to him, anxiously watching him. Outside on the terrace,* JOSHUA *is going through baseball motions, coached by* JOSEPH. *From time to time they move out of sight, reappear, move off again.*

FANNY
(*Playing a card*)

One.

BODO
(*After a minute, to* TECK)
The arrangement of this heating pad grows more complex.

TECK
(*Smiles, moves on the cribbage board*)
And the more wires you remove, the more complex it will grow.

69

BODO

(*Points to bag*)

Man has learned to make man comfortable. Yet all cannot have the comforts. (*To* ANISE) How much did this cost you?

ANISE

It cost me ten dollar. And you have made a ruin of it.

BODO

That is not yet completely true. (*To* FANNY) Did I not install for you a twenty-five-cent button-push for your radio?

TECK

(*Playing a card*)

Two and two. (*Moves pegs on the cribbage board.*)

FANNY

Yes, you're quite an installer.

BODO

(*To* TECK)

As I was wishing to tell you, Count de Brancovis, comfort and plenty exist. Yet all cannot have it. Why?

TECK

I do not know. It has worried many men. Why?

ANISE
(*To* BODO)

Yes, why?

BODO

(*Takes a deep breath, raises his finger as if about to lecture*)
Why? (*Considers a moment, then deflates himself*) I am not as yet sure.

ANISE

I thought not.

FANNY

(*Turns to look at* JOSHUA *and* JOSEPH *on the terrace*)
Would you mind doing that dancing some place else?

JOSEPH
(*Looking in*)

Yes'm. That ain't dancing. I'm teaching Josh baseball.

FANNY

Then maybe he'd teach you how to clean the silver.

JOSEPH

I'm a good silver-cleaner, Miss Fanny.

FANNY

But you're getting out of practice.

JOSEPH
(*After a moment's thought*)
Yes'm. I see what you mean. (*He exits.*)

FANNY
(*Playing a card*)
Three.

JOSHUA
It is my fault. I'm crazy about baseball.

BODO
Baseball players are among the most exploited people in this country. I read about it.

FANNY
You never should have learned to read.

BODO
Their exploited condition is foundationed on the fact that—

JOSHUA
(*Bored*)
All right, all right. I still like baseball.

SARA
Founded, Bodo, not foundationed.

72

JOSHUA

He does it always. He likes long words. In all languages.

TECK

How many languages do you children speak?

BODO

Oh, we do not really know any very well, except German and English. We speak bad French and—

SARA

And bad Danish and bad Czech.

TECK

You seem to have stayed close to the borders of Germany. Did Herr Müller have hopes, as so many did, that National Socialism would be overthrown on every tomorrow?

SARA

We have not given up that hope. Have you, Count de Brancovis?

TECK

I never had it.

JOSHUA

(*Pleasantly*)

Then it must be most difficult for you to sleep.

73

TECK

I beg your pardon?

SARA

Schweig doch, Joshua!

FANNY
(*To* TECK)
Sara told Joshua to shut up. (*Playing a card*) Twelve.

TECK

I have offended you, Mrs. Müller. I am most sorry.

SARA
(*Pleasantly*)
No, sir, you haven't offended me. I just don't like polite political conversations any more.

TECK
(*Nods*)
All of us, in Europe, had too many of them.

SARA

Yes. Too much talk. By this time all of us must know where we are and what we have to do. It's an indulgence to sit in a room and discuss your beliefs as if they were a juicy piece of gossip.

FANNY

You know, Sara, I find it very pleasant that Kurt, considering his history, doesn't make platform speeches. He hasn't tried to convince anybody of anything.

SARA
(*Smiles*)

Why should he, Mama? You are quite old enough to have your own convictions—or Papa's.

FANNY
(*Turns to look at her*)

I am proud to have Papa's convictions.

SARA

Of course. But it might be well to have a few new ones, now and then.

FANNY
(*Peers over at her*)

Are you criticizing me?

SARA
(*Smiles*)

Certainly not.

BABETTE
(*Comes running in from the right entrance door. She has on an apron and she is carrying a plate. She goes to* FANNY)

Eat it while it's hot, Grandma.

(FANNY *peers down, takes the fork, begins to eat.* ANISE
and BODO *both rise, move to* FANNY, *inspect the plate.*)

FANNY

(*To them*)

Go away.

ANISE

It is a potato pancake.

FANNY

And the first good one I've eaten in many, many years.
I love a good potato pancake.

BODO

I likewise.

BABETTE

I am making a great number for dinner. Move away,
Bodo.

TECK

(*Playing a card*)

Fifteen and two.

ANISE

(*Who has followed* BODO *back to the chair*)
You've ruined it! I shall sue you.

JOSHUA

I told you not to let him touch it.

76

SARA

(*Laughs*)

I remember you were always saying that, Anise—that you were going to sue. That's very French. I was sick once in Paris, and Babbie stayed up for a whole night and day and finished a dress I was making for a woman on the Rue Jacob. I told her to tell the woman she'd done it—I thought perhaps the woman would give her a candy or something—and anyway, I was very proud of her work. But no. The woman admitted the dress was well done, but said she was going to sue because I hadn't done it myself. Fancy that.

FANNY

(*Slowly*)

You sewed for a living?

SARA

Not a very good one. But Babbie and I made a little something now and then. Didn't we, darling?

FANNY

(*Sharply*)

Really, Sara, were these—these things necessary? Why couldn't you have written?

SARA

(*Laughs*)

You've asked me that a hundred times in the last week.

JOSHUA
(*Gently*)

I think it is only that Grandma feels sorry for us. Grandma has not seen much of the world.

FANNY

Don't you start giving me lectures, Joshua. I'm fond of you. And of you, Babbie. (*To* ANISE) Are there two desserts for dinner? And are they sweet?

ANISE

Yes.

FANNY
(*Turns to* BODO)

I wish I were fond of you.

BODO

You are. (*Happily*) You are very fond of me.

FANNY
(*Playing a card*)

Twenty-five.

BABETTE

This is for you, Grandma. I'm making a bed-jacket. It is nice lace. Papa brought it to me from Spain and I mean for you to have it.

FANNY
(*Kisses* BABETTE)

Thank you, darling. A sequence and three. A pair and five.

78

(*To* TECK, *as they finish the cribbage game*) There. That's two dollars off. I owe you eight-fifty.

TECK

Let us carry it until tomorrow. You shall give it to me as a going-away token.

FANNY
(*Too pleased*)

You're going away?

TECK
(*Laughs*)

Ah, Madame Fanny. Do not sound *that* happy.

FANNY

Did I? That's rude of me. When are you going?

TECK

In a few days, I think. (*Turns to look at* SARA) We're too many refugees, eh, Mrs. Müller?

SARA
(*Pleasantly*)

Perhaps.

TECK

Will you be leaving, also?

SARA

I beg your pardon?

TECK

I thought perhaps you, too, would be moving on. Herr Müller does not give me the feeling of a man who settles down. Men who have done his work, seldom leave it. Not for a quiet country house.

(*All three children look up.*)

SARA

(*Very quietly*)

What work do you think my husband has done, Count de Brancovis?

TECK

Engineering?

SARA

(*Slowly*)

Yes. Engineering.

FANNY

(*Very deliberately to* TECK)

I don't know what you're saying. They shall certainly not be leaving—ever. Is that understood, Sara?

SARA

Well, Mama—

FANNY

There are no wells about it. You've come home to see me die and you will wait until I'm ready.

80

SARA

(*Laughs*)

Really, Mama, that isn't the reason I came home.

FANNY

It's a good enough reason. I shall do a fine death. I intend to be a great deal of trouble to everybody.

ANISE

I daresay.

FANNY

I shall take to my bed early and stay for years. In great pain.

ANISE

I am sure of it. You will duplicate the disgrace of the birth of Miss Sara.

SARA

(*Laughs*)

Was I born in disgrace?

ANISE

It was not your fault. But it was disgusting. Three weeks before you were to come—all was excellent, of course, in so healthy a woman as Madame Fanny—a great dinner was given here and, most unexpectedly, attended by a beautiful lady from England.

FANNY

Do be still. You are dull and fanciful—

ANISE

Mr. Joshua made the great error of waltzing the beauty for two dances, Madame Fanny being unfitted for the waltz and under no circumstances being the most graceful of dancers.

FANNY

(*Her voice rising*)

Are you crazy? I danced magnificently.

ANISE

It is well you thought so. A minute did not elapse between the second of the waltzes and a scream from Madame Fanny. She was in labor. Two hundred people, and if we had left her alone, she would have remained in the ballroom—

FANNY

How you invent! How you invent!

ANISE

Do not call to me that I am a liar. For three weeks you are in the utmost agony—

FANNY

And so I was. I remember it to this day—

ANISE

(*To* SARA, *angrily*)

Not a pain. Not a single pain. She would lie up there in state, stealing candy from herself. Then, when your Papa would rest himself for a minute at the dinner or with a book, a scream would dismantle the house—it was revolting. (*Spitefully to* FANNY) And now the years have passed and I may disclose to you that Mr. Joshua knew you were going through the play-acting—

FANNY
(*Rises*)
He did not. You are a malicious—

ANISE
Once he said to me, "Anise, it is well that I am in love. This is of a great strain and her Great-uncle Freddie was not right in the head, neither."

FANNY
(*Screaming*)
You will leave this house— You are a liar, a woman of—

SARA
Mama, sit down.

ANISE
I will certainly leave this house. I will—

SARA
(*Sharply*)
Both of you. Sit down. And be still.

ANISE
She has intimated that I lie—

FANNY
(*Screaming*)
Intimated! Is that what I was doing— (ANISE *begins to leave the room*) All right. I beg your pardon. I apologize.

(ANISE *turns*.)

SARA

Both of you. You are acting like children.

BODO

Really, Mama. You insult us.

ANISE

I accept your apology. Seat yourself.

(*They both sit down*.)

FANNY
(*After a silence*)
I am unloved.

BABETTE

I love you, Grandma.

FANNY

Do you, Babbie?

JOSHUA

And I.

FANNY

(*Nods, very pleased. To* BODO)

And you?

BODO

I loved you the primary second I saw you.

FANNY

You are a charlatan.

ANISE

As for me, I am fond of all the living creatures. It is true that the children cause me greater work, which in turn more greatly inconveniences the feet. However, I do not complain. I believe in children.

FANNY

Rather like believing in the weather, isn't it? (DAVID *and* KURT *come in from the terrace. Both are in work clothes, their sleeves rolled up*) Where have you been?

DAVID

Oh, we've been helping Mr. Chabeuf spray the fruit trees.

ANISE

Mr. Chabeuf says that Herr Müller has the makings of a good farmer. From a Frenchman that is a large thing to say.

KURT

(*Who has looked around the room, looked at* TECK, *strolled over to* BODO)

Mr. Chabeuf and I have an excellent time exchanging mis-

85

information. My father was a farmer. I have a wide knowl-
edge of farmer's misinformation.

FANNY

This is good farm land. Perhaps, in time—

DAVID

(*Laughs*)

Mama would give you the place, Kurt, if you guaranteed
that your great-grandchildren would die here.

KURT

(*Smiles*)

I would like to so guarantee.

TECK

A farmer. That is very interesting. Abandon your ideals,
Herr Müller?

KURT

Ideals? (*Carefully*) Sara, heisst das auf deutsch "Ideale"?

SARA

Yes.

KURT

Is that what I have now? I do not like the word. It gives
to me the picture of a small, pale man at a seaside resort.
(*To* BODO) What are you doing?

86

BODO

Preparing an elderly electric pad for Miss Anise. I am confused.

KURT

(*Wanders toward the piano*)

So it seems.

BODO

Something has gone wrong with the principle on which I have been working. It is probably that I will ask your assistance.

KURT

(*Bows to him*)

Thank you. Whenever you are ready. (*Begins to pick out notes with one hand.*)

FANNY

We shall have a little concert tomorrow evening. In honor of Babbie's birthday. (*To* KURT) Kurt, you and I will play "The Clock Symphony." Then Joshua and I will play the duet we've learned, and Babbie will sing. And I shall finish with a Chopin Nocturne.

DAVID

(*Laughs*)

I thought you'd be the last on the program.

TECK

Where is Marthe?

FANNY

She'll be back soon. She went into town to do an errand for me. (*To* DAVID) Did you buy presents for everybody?

DAVID

I did.

SARA

(*Smiles, to* BABETTE)

We always did that here. If somebody had a birthday, we all got presents. Nice, isn't it?

DAVID

(*To* ANISE)

I shall buy you an electric pad. You will need it.

ANISE

Indeed.

FANNY

Did you buy me a good present?

DAVID

Pretty good. (*Pats* BABETTE's *head*) The best present goes to Babbie; it's *her* birthday.

FANNY

Jewelry?

DAVID

No, not jewelry.

FANNY

Oh. Not jewelry.

DAVID

Why? Why should you want jewelry? You've got too many bangles now.

FANNY

I didn't say I wanted it. I just asked you.

TECK

(*Gets up*)

It was a natural mistake, David. You see, Mrs. Mellie Sewell told your mother that she had seen you and Marthe in Barstow's. And your mother said you were probably buying her a present, or one for Babbie.

DAVID

(*Too sharply*)

Yes.

TECK

(*Laughs*)

Yes what?

DAVID

(*Slowly*)

Just yes.

FANNY

(*Too hurriedly*)

Mellie gets everything wrong. She's very anxious to meet Marthe because she used to know Francie Cabot, her aunt. Marthe's aunt, I mean, not Mellie's.

SARA

(*Too hurriedly*)

She really came to inspect Kurt and me. But I saw her

89

first. (*She looks anxiously at* DAVID, *who has turned his back on the room and is facing the terrace*) You were lucky to be out, David.

DAVID

Oh, she calls every Saturday afternoon, to bring Mama all the Washington gossip of the preceding week. She gets it all wrong, you understand, but that doesn't make any difference to either Mama or her. Mama then augments it, wits it up, Papa used to say—

FANNY

Certainly. I sharpen it a little. Mellie has no sense of humor.

DAVID

So Mama sharpens it a little, and delivers it tomorrow afternoon to old lady Marcy down the road. Old lady Marcy hasn't heard a word in ten years, so she unsharpens it again, and changes the names. By Wednesday afternoon—

TECK
(*Smiles*)

By Wednesday afternoon it will not be you who were in Barstow's, and it will be a large diamond pin with four sapphires delivered to Gaby Deslys.

DAVID
(*Turns, looks at him*)

Exactly.

FANNY
(*Very nervously*)
Francie Cabot, Marthe's aunt, you understand— (*To* KURT)
Did you ever know Paul von Seitz, a German?

KURT
I have heard of him.

FANNY
(*Speaking very rapidly*)
Certainly. He was your Ambassador to somewhere, I've
forgotten. Well, Francie Cabot married him. I could have.
Any American, not crippled, whose father had money— He
was crazy about me. I was better-looking than Francie. Well,
years later when he was your Ambassador—my father was,
too, as you probably know—not your Ambassador, of course,
ours—but I am talking about Von Seitz.

DAVID
(*Laughs to* KURT)
You can understand how it goes. Old lady Marcy is not en-
tirely to blame.

FANNY
Somebody asked me if I didn't regret not marrying him. I
said, "Madame, je le regrette tous les jours et j'en suis
heureuse chaque soir." (FANNY *turns to* DAVID) That means
I regret it every day and am happy about it every night. You
understand what I meant, by *night?* Styles in wit change so.

91

DAVID

I understood it, Mama.

JOSHUA

We, too, Grandma.

BABETTE

(*Approvingly*)

It is most witty.

BODO

I do not know that I understood. You will explain to me, Grandma?

SARA

Later.

FANNY

(*Turns to look at* TECK)

You remember the old Paul von Seitz?

TECK

(*Nods*)

He was stationed in Paris when I first was there.

FANNY

Of course. I always forget you were a diplomat.

TECK

It is just as well.

FANNY

There's something insane about a Roumanian diplomat.

Pure insane. I knew another one, once. He wanted to marry me, too.

SARA
(*Laughs*)

All of Europe.

FANNY

Not all. Some. Naturally. I was rich, I was witty, my family was of the best. I was handsome, unaffected—

DAVID

And noble and virtuous and kind and elegant and fashionable and simple—it's hard to remember everything you were. I've often thought it must have been boring for Papa to have owned such perfection.

FANNY
(*Shrieks*)

What! Your father bored with me! Not for a second of our life—

DAVID
(*Laughs*)

Oh God, when will I learn?

BODO

Do not shriek, Grandma. It is an unpleasant sound for the ear.

FANNY

Where was I? Oh, yes. What I started out to say was— (*She turns, speaks carefully to* TECK) Mellie Sewell told me, when you left the room, that she had heard from Louis Chandler's child's governess that you had won quite a bit of money in a poker game with Sam Chandler and some Germans at the Embassy. (KURT, *who has been playing the piano, stops playing very abruptly.* TECK *turns to look at him*) *That's* how I thought of Von Seitz. His nephew Philip was in on the game.

DAVID
(*Looks at* TECK)
It must have been a big game. Sam Chandler plays in big games.

TECK
Not big enough.

DAVID
Have you known Sam long?

TECK
For years. Every Embassy in Europe knew him.

DAVID
(*Sharply*)
Sam and Nazis must make an unpleasant poker game.

(KURT *begins to play a new melody.*)

TECK
(*Who has not looked away from* KURT)
I do not play poker to be amused.

94

DAVID

(*Irritably*)

What's Sam selling now?

TECK

Bootleg munitions. He always has.

DAVID

You don't mind?

TECK

Mind? I have not thought about it.

FANNY

Well, you ought to think about it. Sam Chandler has always been a scoundrel. All the Chandlers are. They're cousins of mine. Mama used to say they never should have learned to walk on two feet. They would have been more comfortable on four.

TECK

Do you know the young Von Seitz, Herr Müller? He was your military attaché in Spain.

KURT

He was the German government attaché in Spain. I know his name, of course. He is a famous artillery expert. But the side on which I fought was not where he was stationed, Count de Brancovis.

ANISE

(BABETTE *and* JOSHUA *begin to hum the song* KURT *is playing.* SARA *begins to hum*)

It is time for the bath and the change of clothes. I will give you five more minutes—

FANNY

What is the song?

TECK

It was a German soldier's song. They sang it as they straggled back in '18. I remember hearing it in Berlin. Were you there then, Herr Müller?

KURT

(*The playing and the humming continue*)

I was not in Berlin.

TECK

But you were in the war, of course?

KURT

Yes. I was in the war.

FANNY

You didn't think then you'd live to see another war.

KURT

Many of us were afraid we would.

96

FANNY

What are the words?

SARA

The Germans in Spain, in Kurt's Brigade, wrote new words for the song.

KURT

This was what you heard in Berlin, in 1918. (*Begins to sing in German.*)

"Wir zieh'n Heim, wir zieh'n Heim,
Mancher kommt nicht mit,
Mancher ging verschütt,
Aber Freunde sind wir stets."
(*In English.*)
"We come home. We come home.
Some of us are gone, and some of us are lost, but
we are friends:
Our blood is on the earth together.
Some day. Some day we shall meet again.
Farewell."

(*Stops singing*) At a quarter before six on the morning of November 7th, 1936, eighteen years later, five hundred Germans walked through the Madrid streets on their way to defend the Manzanares River. We felt good that morning. You know how it is to be good when it is needed to be good? So we had need of new words to say that. I translate with awkwardness, you understand. (*Begins to sing in English.*)

"And so we have met again.
The blood did not have time to dry.
We lived to stand and fight again.
This time we fight for people.
This time the bastards will keep their hands away.
Those who sell the blood of other men, this time,
They keep their hands away.
For us to stand.
For us to fight.
This time, no farewell, no farewell."

(*Music dies out. There is silence for a minute.*)
We did not win. (*Looks up, gently.*) It would have been a different world if we had.

SARA

Papa said so years ago. Do you remember, Mama? "For every man who lives without freedom, the rest of us must face the guilt."

FANNY

Yes. "We are liable in the conscience-balance for the tailor in Lodz, the black man in our South, the peasant in—" (*Turns to* TECK. *Unpleasantly*) Your country, I think.

ANISE
(*Rises*)

Come. Baths for everybody. (*To* BODO) Gather the wires. You have wrecked my cure.

BODO

If you would allow me a few minutes more—

ANISE

Come along. I have been duped for long enough. Come Joshua. Babette. Baths.

JOSHUA

(*Starts out after* ANISE. BABETTE *begins to gather up her sewing*)

My tub is a thing of glory. But I do not like it so prepared for me and so announced by Miss Anise. (*He exits.*)

BODO

(*To* ANISE)

You are angry about this. I do not blame you with my heart or my head. I admit I have failed. But Papa will repair it, Anise. Will you not, Papa? In a few minutes—

TECK

(*To* BODO)

Your father is an expert electrician?

BODO

Oh yes, sir.

TECK

And as good with radio—

(BODO *begins to nod.*)

KURT

(*Sharply*)

Count de Brancovis. Make your questions to me, please. Not to my children.

(*The others look up, surprised.*)

TECK

(*Pleasantly*)

Very well, Herr Müller.

ANISE

(*As she exits with* BODO)

Nobody can fix it. You have made a pudding of it.

BODO

(*As he follows her*)

Do not worry. In five minutes tonight, you will have a pad far better— (*As* BODO *reaches the door he bumps into* MARTHE *who is carrying large dress boxes*) Oh. Your pardon. Oh, hello. (*He disappears.*)

MARTHE

(*Gaily*)

Hello. (*To* FANNY) I waited for them. I was afraid they wouldn't deliver this late in the day. (*To* SARA) Come on, Sara. I can't wait to see them.

SARA

What?

MARTHE

Dresses. From Fanny. A tan linen, and a dark green with wonderful buttons, a white net for Babbie, and a suit for you, and play dresses for Babbie, and a dinner dress in gray to wear for Babbie's birthday—gray should be good for you, Sara—all from Savitt's. We sneaked the measurements, Anise and I—

SARA

(*She goes toward* FANNY)

How nice of you, Mama. How very kind of you. And of you, Marthe, to take so much trouble— (*She leans down, kisses* FANNY) You're a sweet woman, Mama.

DAVID

That's the first time Mama's ever heard that word. (*He takes the boxes from* MARTHE, *puts them near the staircase.* MARTHE *smiles at him, touches his hand, as* TECK *watches them.*)

FANNY

(*Giggles*)

I have a bottom sweetness, if you understand what I mean.

DAVID

I have been too close to the bottom to see it.

FANNY

That should be witty. I don't know why it isn't.

(BABETTE *goes over to stare at the boxes.*)

SARA

From Savitt's. Extravagant of you. They had such lovely clothes. I remember my coming-out dress— (*Goes to* KURT) Do you remember the black suit with the braid, and the Milan hat? Not the *first* day we met, but the picnic day? (*He smiles up at her*) Well, they were from Savitt's. That was over twenty years ago— I've known you a long time. Me, in an evening dress. Now you'll have to take me into Washington. I want to show off. Next week, and we'll dance, maybe— (*Sees that he is not looking at her*) What's the matter, darling? (*No answer. Slowly he turns to look at her*) What's the matter, Kurt? (*Takes his arms, very unhappily*) What have I done? It isn't that dresses have ever mattered to me, it's just that—

KURT

Of course, they have mattered to you. As they should. I do not think of the dress. (*Draws her to him*) How many years have I loved that face?

SARA

(*Her face very happy*)

So?

KURT

So. (*He leans down, kisses her, as if it were important.*)

SARA

(*Pleased, unembarrassed*)

There are other people here.

MARTHE

(*Slowly*)

And good for us to see.

TECK

Nostalgia?

MARTHE

No. Nostalgia is for something you have known.

(FANNY *coughs.*)

BABETTE

(*Comes to* FANNY)

Grandma, is it allowed to look at my dresses?

FANNY

Of course, child. Run along.

BABETTE

(*Picks up the boxes, goes toward the hall entrance, stops near* FANNY)

I love dresses, I have a great fondness for materials and colors. Thank you, Grandma. (*She runs out of the room.*)

(JOSEPH *appears in the doorway.*)

JOSEPH

There is a long-distance operator with a long-distance call for Mr. Müller. She wants to talk with him on the long-distance phone.

KURT

Oh— Excuse me, please—

(KURT *rises quickly.* SARA *turns sharply to look at him.* TECK *looks up.* KURT *goes quickly out.* TECK *watches him go.* SARA *stands staring after him.*)

MARTHE

(*Laughs*)

I feel the same way as Babbie. Come on, Sara. Let's try them on.

(SARA *does not turn.*)

TECK

You also have a new dress?

MARTHE

(*Looks at him*)

Yes. Fanny was kind to me, too.

TECK

You are a very generous woman, Madame Fanny. Did you also give her a sapphire bracelet from Barstow's?

FANNY

I beg your—

DAVID

(*Slowly*)

No. I gave Marthe the bracelet. And I understand that it is not any business of yours.

(FANNY *rises*. SARA *turns*.)

FANNY

Really, David—

DAVID

Be still, Mama.

TECK

(*After a second*)

Did you tell him that, Marthe?

MARTHE

Yes.

TECK

(*Looks up at her*)

I shall not forgive you for that. (*Looks at* DAVID) It is a

105

statement which no man likes to hear from another man. You understand that? (*Playfully*) That is the type of thing about which we used to play at duels in Europe.

DAVID

(*Comes toward him*)

We are not so musical comedy here. And you are not in Europe.

TECK

Even if I were, I would not suggest any such action. I would have reasons for not wishing it.

DAVID

It would be well for you not to suggest *any* action. And the reason for *that* is you might get hurt.

TECK

(*Slowly*)

That would not be my reason. (*To* MARTHE) Your affair has gone far enough—

MARTHE

(*Sharply*)

It is not an affair—

TECK

I do not care what it is. The time has come to leave here. Go upstairs and pack your things. (*She does not move.* DAVID *turns toward her*) Go on, Marthe.

MARTHE
(*To* DAVID)

I am not going with him. I told you that.

DAVID

I don't want you to go with him.

FANNY
(*Carefully*)

Really, David, aren't you interfering in all this a good deal—

DAVID
(*Carefully*)

Yes, Mama. I am.

TECK
(*To* MARTHE)

When you are speaking to me, please say what you have to say to me.

MARTHE
(*Comes to him*)

You are trying to frighten me. But you are not going to frighten me any more. I will say it to you: I am not going with you. I am never going with you again.

TECK
(*Softly*)

If you do not fully mean what you say, or if you might change your mind, you are talking unwisely, Marthe.

MARTHE

I know that.

TECK

Shall we talk about it alone?

MARTHE

You can't make me go, can you, Teck?

TECK

No, I can't make you.

MARTHE

Then there's no sense talking about it.

TECK

Are you in love with him?

MARTHE

Yes.

FANNY

(*Sharply*)

Marthe! What is all this?

MARTHE

(*Sharply*)

I'll tell *you* about it in a minute.

DAVID

You don't have to explain anything to **anybody**.

TECK
(Ignores him)

Is he in love with you?

MARTHE

I don't think so. You won't believe it, because you can't believe anything that hasn't got tricks to it, but David hasn't much to do with this. I told you I would leave some day, and I remember where I said it—*(Slowly)*—and why I said it.

TECK

I also remember. But I did not believe you. I have not had much to offer you these last years. But if now we had some money and could go back—

MARTHE

No. I don't like you, Teck. I never have.

TECK

And I have always known it.

FANNY
(Stiffly)

I think your lack of affections should be discussed with more privacy. Perhaps—

DAVID

Mama—

MARTHE

There is nothing to discuss. Strange. I've talked to myself about this scene for almost fifteen years. I knew a lot of things to say to you and I used to lie awake at night or walk along the street and say them. Now I don't want to. I guess you only want to talk that way, when you're not sure what you can do. When you're sure, then what's the sense of saying it? "This is why and this is why and this—" (*Very happily*) But when you know you can do it, you don't have to say anything; you can just go. And I'm going. There is nothing you can do. I would like you to believe that now.

TECK

Very well, Marthe. I think I made a mistake. I should not have brought you here. I believe you now.

MARTHE

(*After a pause, she looks at* DAVID)
I'll move into Washington, and—

DAVID

Yes. Later. But I'd like you to stay here for a while, with us, if you wouldn't mind.

SARA

It would be better for you, Marthe—

FANNY

It's very interesting that I am not being consulted about

this. (*To* MARTHE) I have nothing against you, Marthe. I am sorry for you, but I don't think—

MARTHE

Thank you, Sara, David. But I'd rather move in now. (*Turns, comes toward* FANNY) But perhaps I have something against you. Do you remember my wedding?

FANNY

Yes.

MARTHE

Do you remember how pleased Mama was with herself? Brilliant Mama, handsome Mama—everybody thought so, didn't they? A seventeen-year-old daughter, marrying a pretty good title, about to secure herself in a world that Mama liked —she didn't ask me what I liked. And the one time I tried to tell her, she frightened me— (*Looks up*) Maybe I've always been frightened. All my life.

TECK

Of course.

MARTHE

(*To* FANNY, *as if she had not heard* TECK)

I remember Mama's face at the wedding—it was *her* wedding, really, not mine.

FANNY

(*Sharply*)

You are very hard on your mother.

III

MARTHE

Nineteen hundred and twenty-five. No, I'm not hard on her. I only tell the truth. She wanted a life for me, I suppose. It just wasn't the life I wanted for myself. (*Sharply*) And that's what you have tried to do. With your children. In another way. Only Sara got away. And that made you angry —until so many years went by that you forgot.

FANNY

I don't usually mind people saying anything they think, but I find that—

MARTHE

I don't care what you mind or don't mind. I'm in love with your son—

FANNY
(*Very sharply*)

That's unfortunate—

MARTHE

And I'm sick of watching you try to make him into his father. I don't think you even know you do it any more and I don't think he knows it any more, either. And that's what's most dangerous about it.

FANNY
(*Very angrily*)

I don't know what you are talking about.

112

DAVID

I think you do. (*Smiles*) You shouldn't mind hearing the truth—and neither should I.

FANNY
(*Worried, sharply*)

David! What does all this nonsense mean? I—

MARTHE
(*To* FANNY)

Look. That pretty world Mama got me into was a tough world, see? I'm used to trouble. So don't try to interfere with me, because I won't let you. (*She goes to* DAVID) Let's just have a good time. (*He leans down, takes both her hands, kisses them. Then slowly, she turns away, starts to exit. To* TECK) You will also be going today?

TECK

Yes.

MARTHE

Then let us make sure we go in different directions, and do not meet again. Good-bye, Teck.

TECK

Good-bye, Marthe. You will not believe me, but I tried my best, and I am now most sorry to lose you.

MARTHE

Yes. I believe you. (*She moves out. There is silence for a minute.*)

FANNY

Well, a great many things have been said in the last few minutes.

DAVID

(*Crosses to bell cord. To* TECK)

I will get Joseph to pack for you.

TECK

Thank you. Do not bother. I will ring for him when I am ready. (KURT *comes in from the study door.* SARA *turns, stares at him, waits. He does not look at her*) It will not take me very long. (*He starts for the door, looking at* KURT.)

SARA

What is it, Kurt?

KURT

It is nothing of importance, darling— (*He looks quickly at* TECK, *who is moving very slowly.*)

SARA

Don't tell me it's nothing. I know the way you look when—

KURT

(*Sharply*)

I said it was of no importance. I must get to California for a few weeks. That is all.

114

SARA

I—

TECK

(*Turns*)

It is in the afternoon newspaper, Herr Müller. (*Points to paper on table*) I was waiting to find the proper moment to call it to your attention. (*He moves toward the table, as they all turn to watch him. He picks up the paper, turns it over, begins to read*) "Zurich, Switzerland: The Zurich papers today reprinted a despatch from the *Berliner Tageblatt*—on the capture of Colonel Max Freidank. Freidank is said—(SARA *begins to move toward him*)—to be the chief of the Anti-Nazi Underground Movement. Colonel Freidank has long been an almost legendary figure. The son of the famous General Freidank, he was a World War officer and a distinguished physicist before the advent of Hitler." That is all.

SARA

Max—

KURT

Be still, Sara.

TECK

They told me of it at the Embassy last night. They also told me that with him, they had taken a man who called himself Ebber, and a man who called himself Triste. They could not find a man called Gotter. (*He starts again toward the door*) I shall be a lonely man without Marthe. I am also a very poor one. I should like to have ten thousand dollars before I go.

DAVID

(*Carefully*)

You will make no loans in this house.

TECK

I was not speaking of a loan.

FANNY

(*Carefully*)

God made you not only a scoundrel but a fool. That is a dangerous combination.

DAVID

(*Suddenly leaps toward* TECK)

Damn you, you—

KURT

(*Suddenly pounds on the top of the piano, as* DAVID *almost reaches* TECK)

Leave him alone. (*Moves quickly to stop* DAVID) Leave him alone! *David! Leave him alone!*

DAVID

(*Angrily to* KURT)

Keep out of it. (*Starts toward* TECK *again*) I'm beginning to see what Marthe meant. Blackmailing with your wife— You—

KURT

(*Very sharply*)

He is not speaking of his wife. Or you. He means me. (*Looks at* TECK) Is that correct?

(SARA *moves toward* KURT. DAVID *draws back, bewildered*.)

TECK

Good. It was necessary for me to hear you say it. You understand that?

KURT

I understand it.

SARA
(*Frightened, softly*)

Kurt—

DAVID

What is all this about? What the hell are you talking about?

TECK
(*Sharply for the first time*)

Be still. (*To* KURT) At your convenience. Your hands are shaking, Herr Müller.

KURT
(*Quietly*)

My hands were broken: they are bad when I have fear.

TECK

I am sorry. I can understand that. It is not pleasant. (*Motions toward* FANNY *and* DAVID) Perhaps you would like a little time to— I will go and pack, and be ready to leave. We will all find that more comfortable, I think. You should get yourself a smaller gun, Herr Müller. That pistol you have been carrying is big and awkward.

KURT

You saw the pistol when you examined our bags?

TECK

You knew that?

KURT

Oh, yes. I have the careful eye, through many years of needing it. And then you have not the careful eye. The pistol was lying to the left of a paper package and when you leave, it is to the right of the package.

SARA

Kurt! Do you mean that—

KURT

(*Sharply*)

Please, darling, do not do that.

TECK

It is a German Army Luger?

KURT

Yes.

TECK

Keep it in your pocket, Herr Müller. You will have no need to use it. And, in any case, I am not afraid of it. You understand that?

KURT
(Slowly)

I understand that you are not a man of fears. That is strange to me, because I am a man who has so many fears.

TECK
(Laughs, as he exits)

Are you? That is most interesting. (*He exits.*)

DAVID
(Softly)

What is this about, Kurt?

KURT

He knows who I am and what I do and what I carry with me.

SARA
(Carefully)

What about Max?

KURT

The telephone was from Mexico. Ilse received a cable. Early on the morning of Monday, they caught Ebber and Triste. An hour after they took Max in Berlin. (*She looks up at him, begins to shake her head. He presses her arm*) Yes. It is hard.

FANNY
(Softly)

You said he knew who you were and what you carried with you. I don't understand.

KURT

I am going to tell you: I am a German outlaw. I work with many others in an illegal organization. I have so worked for seven years. I am on what is called a desired list. But I did not know I was worth ten thousand dollars. My price has risen.

DAVID

(*Slowly*)

And what do you carry with you?

KURT

Twenty-three thousand dollars. It has been gathered from the pennies and the nickels of the poor who do not like Fascism, and who believe in the work we do. I came here to bring Sara home and to get the money. I had hopes to rest here for a while, and then—

SARA

(*Slowly*)

And I had hopes someone else would take it back and you would stay with us— (*Shakes her head, then*) Max is not dead?

KURT

No. The left side of his face is dead. (*Softly*) It was a good face.

SARA

(*To* FANNY *and* DAVID, *as if she were going to cry*)

It was a very good face. He and Kurt—in the old days—

(*To* KURT) After so many years. If Max got caught, then nobody's got a chance. Nobody. (*She suddenly sits down.*)

DAVID
(*Points upstairs*)
He wants to sell what he knows to you? Is that right?

KURT
Yes.

FANNY
Wasn't it careless of you to leave twenty-three thousand
dollars lying around to be seen?

KURT
No, it was not careless of me. It is in a locked brief-case.
I have thus carried money for many years. There seemed no
safer place than Sara's home. It was careless of you to have
in your house a man who opens baggage and blackmails.

DAVID
(*Sharply*)
Yes. It was very careless.

FANNY
But you said you knew he'd seen it—

KURT
Yes. I knew it the first day we were here. What was I to

do about it? He is not a man who steals. This is a safer method. I knew that it would come some other way. I have been waiting to see what the way would be. That is all I could do.

DAVID
(*To* FANNY)

What's the difference? It's been done. (*To* KURT) If he wants to sell to you, he must have another buyer. Who?

KURT

The Embassy. Von Seitz, I think.

DAVID

You mean he has told Von Seitz about you and—

KURT

No. I do not think he has told him anything. As yet. It would be foolish of him. He has probably only asked most guarded questions.

DAVID

But you're here. You're in this country. They can't do anything to you. They wouldn't be crazy enough to try it. Is your passport all right?

KURT

Not quite.

FANNY

Why not? Why isn't it?

KURT

(*Wearily, as if he were bored*)

Because people like me are not given visas with such ease. And I was in a hurry to bring my wife and my children to safety. (*Sharply*) Madame Fanny, you must come to understand it is no longer the world you once knew.

DAVID

It doesn't matter. You're a political refugee. We don't turn back people like you. People who are in danger. You will give me your passport and tomorrow morning I'll see Barens. We'll tell him the truth— (*Points to the door*) Tell de Brancovis to go to hell. There's not a damn thing he or anybody else can do.

SARA

(*Looks up at* KURT, *who is staring at her*)

You don't understand, David.

DAVID

There's a great deal I don't understand. But there's nothing to worry about.

SARA

Not much to worry about as long as Kurt is in this house. But he's not going to—

KURT

The Count has made the guess that—

SARA

That you will go back to get Ebber and Triste and Max. Is that right, Kurt? Is that right?

KURT

Yes, darling, I will try. They were taken to Sonnenburg. Guards can be bribed— It has been done once before at Sonnenburg. We will try for it again. I must go back, Sara. I must start.

SARA

Of course, you must go back. I guess I was trying to think it wouldn't come. But— (*To* FANNY *and* DAVID) Kurt's got to go back. He's got to go home. He's got to buy them out. He'll do it, too. You'll see. (*She stops, breathes*) It's hard enough to get back. Very hard. But if they knew he was coming— They want Kurt bad. Almost as much as they wanted Max— And then there are hundreds of others, too— (*She gets up, comes to him. He holds her, puts his face in her hair. She stands holding him, trying to speak without crying. She puts her face down on his head*) Don't be scared, darling. You'll get back. You'll see. You've done it before— you'll do it again. Don't be scared. You'll get Max out all right. (*Gasps*) And then you'll do his work, won't you? That's good. That's fine. You'll do a good job, the way you've always done. (*She is crying very hard. To* FANNY) Kurt doesn't feel well. He was wounded and he gets tired— (*To* KURT) You don't feel well, do you? (*Slowly. She is crying too hard now to be heard clearly*) Don't be scared, darling. You'll get home. Don't worry, you'll get home. Yes, you will.

(*The curtain falls.*)

ACT THREE

ACT THREE

Scene: *The same. A half hour later.*

At Rise: FANNY *is sitting in a chair.* KURT *is at the piano, his head resting on one hand. He is playing softly with the other hand.* SARA *is sitting very quietly on the couch.* DAVID *is pacing on the terrace.*

FANNY
(*To* DAVID)

David, would you stop that pacing, please? (DAVID *comes in*) And would you stop that one-hand piano playing? Either play, or get up.

> (KURT *gets up, crosses to the couch, sits.* SARA *looks at him, gets up, crosses to the decanters, begins to make a drink.*)

SARA
(*To* DAVID)

A drink?

DAVID

What? Yes, please. (*To* KURT) Do you intend to buy your friends out of jail?

KURT

I intend to try.

129

FANNY

It's all very strange to me. I thought things were so well run that bribery and—

KURT

(*Smiles*)

What a magnificent work Fascists have done in convincing the world that they are men from legends.

DAVID

They have done very well for themselves—unfortunately.

KURT

Yes. But not by themselves. Does it make us all uncomfortable to remember that they came in on the shoulders of the most powerful men in the world? Of course. And so we would prefer to believe they are men from the planets. They are not. Let me reassure you. They are smart, they are sick, and they are cruel. But given men who know what they fight for— (*Shrugs*) You saw it in Spain. (*Laughs*) I will console you. A year ago last month, at three o'clock in the morning, Freidank and I, with two elderly pistols, raided the home of the Gestapo chief in Konstanz, got what we wanted and the following morning Freidank was eating his breakfast three blocks away, and I was over the Swiss border.

FANNY

(*Slowly*)

You are brave men.

KURT

I do not tell you the story to prove we are remarkable, but to prove they are *not*.

(SARA *brings him a drink. Gives one to* DAVID.)

SARA

(*Softly, touching* KURT'S *shoulder*)

Kurt loves Max.

KURT

Always since I came here I have a dream: that he will come in this room some day. How he would like it here, eh, Sara? He loves good food and wine, and you have books— (*Laughs happily*) He is fifty-nine years of age. And when he was fifty-seven, he carried me on his back, seven miles across the border. I had been hurt— That takes a man, does it not?

FANNY

(*To* KURT)

You look like a sick man to me.

KURT

No. I'm only tired. I do not like to wait. It will go.

SARA

(*Sharply*)

Oh, it's more than that. This is one of the times you wonder why everything has to go against you.

KURT

Waiting. It is waiting that is bad.

DAVID

(*Points upstairs*)

Damn him! He's doing it deliberately.

KURT

It is then the corruption begins. Once in Spain I waited for two days until the planes would exhaust themselves. I think then why must our side fight always with naked hands. The spirit and the hands. All is against us but ourselves. Sometimes, it was as if you must put up your hands and tear the wings from the planes—and then it is bad.

SARA

You will not think that when the time comes. It will go.

KURT

Of a certainty.

FANNY

But does it have to go on being your hands?

KURT

For each man, his own hands. He has to sleep with them.

DAVID

(*Uncomfortably, as if he did not like to say it*)

That's right. I guess it's the way all of us should feel. But

132

—but you have a family. Isn't there somebody else who hasn't a wife and children—

KURT

Each could have his own excuse. Some love for the first time, some have bullet holes, some have fear of the camps, some are sick, many are getting older. (*Shrugs*) Each could find a reason. And many find it. My children are not the only children in the world, even to me.

FANNY

That's noble of you, of course. But they are your children, nevertheless. And Sara, she—

SARA

Mama—

KURT

(*After a slight pause*)

One means always in English to insult with that word noble?

FANNY

Of course not, I—

KURT

It is not noble. It is the way I must live. Good or bad, it is what I am. (*Turns deliberately to look at* FANNY) And what I am is not what you wanted for your daughter, twenty years ago or now.

FANNY

You are misunderstanding me.

KURT

(*Smiles*)

For our girl, too, we want a safe and happy life. And it is thus I try to make it for her. We each have our way. I do not convert you to mine.

DAVID

You are very certain of your way.

KURT

(*Smiles*)

I seem so to you? Good.

(JOSEPH *appears in the hall doorway. He is carrying valises and overcoats.*)

JOSEPH

What'll I do with these, Miss Fanny?

FANNY

They're too large for eating, aren't they? What were you thinking of doing with them?

JOSEPH

I mean, it's Fred's day off.

DAVID

All right. You drive him into town.

134

JOSEPH

Then who's going to serve at dinner?

FANNY

(*Impatiently*)

Belle can do it alone tonight.

JOSEPH

No she can't. Belle's upstairs packing with Miss Marthe. My, there's quite a lot of departing, ain't there?

FANNY

(*Very impatiently*)

All right, then cook can bring in dinner.

JOSEPH

I wouldn't ask her to do that, if I were you. She's mighty mad: the sink pipe is leaking again. You just better wait for your dinner till I get back from Washington.

FANNY

(*Shouting*)

We are not cripples and we were eating dinner in this house before you arrived to show us how to use the knife and fork. (JOSEPH *laughs*) Go on. Put his things in the car. I'll ring for you when he's ready.

JOSEPH

You told me the next time you screamed to remind you to ask my pardon.

FANNY

You call that screaming?

JOSEPH

Yes'm.

FANNY

Very well. I ask your pardon. (*Waves him away*) Go on!

JOSEPH

Yes'm. (*Exits.*)

(TECK *appears in the door. He is carrying his hat and the brief-case we have seen in Act One.* SARA, *seeing the brief-case, looks startled, looks quickly at* KURT. KURT *watches* TECK *as he comes toward him.* TECK *throws his hat on a chair, comes to the table at which* KURT *is sitting, puts the brief-case on the table.* KURT *puts out his hand, puts it on the brief-case, leaves it there.*)

TECK

(*Smiles at the gesture*)

Nothing has been touched, Herr Müller. I brought it from your room, for your convenience.

136

FANNY
(*Angrily*)
Why didn't you steal it? Since you do not seem to—

TECK
That would have been very foolish of me, Madame Fanny.

KURT
Very.

TECK
I hope I have not kept you waiting too long. I wanted to give you an opportunity to make any explanations—

DAVID
(*Angrily*)
Does your price include listening to this tony conversation?

TECK
(*Turns to look at him*)
My price will rise if I have to spend the next few minutes being interrupted by your temper. I will do my business with Herr Müller. And you will understand, I will take from you no interruptions, no exclamations, no lectures, no opinions of what I am or what I am doing.

KURT
(*Quietly*)
You will not be interrupted.

137

TECK

(*Sits down at table with* KURT)

I have been curious about you, Herr Müller. Even before you came here. Because Fanny and David either knew very little about you, which was strange, or wouldn't talk about you, which was just as strange. Have you ever had come to you one of those insistent half-memories of some person or some place?

KURT

(*Quietly, without looking up*)

You had such a half-memory of me?

TECK

Not even a memory, but something. The curiosity of one European for another, perhaps.

KURT

A most sharp curiosity. You lost no time examining— (*Pats the case*)—this. You are an expert with locks?

TECK

No, indeed. Only when I wish to be.

FANNY

(*Angrily, to* TECK)

I would like you out of this house as quickly as—

TECK

(*Turns to her*)

Madame Fanny, I have just asked Mr. David not to do that. I must now ask you. (*Leans forward to* KURT) Herr Müller, I got one of the desired lists from Von Seitz, without, of course, revealing anything to him. As you probably know, they are quite easy to get. I simply told him that we refugees move in small circles and I might come across somebody on it. If, however, I have to listen to any more of this from any of you, I shall go immediately to him.

KURT

(*To* DAVID *and* FANNY)

Please allow the Count to do this in his own way. It will be best.

TECK

(*Takes a sheet of paper from his pocket*)

There are sixty-three names on this list. I read them carefully, I narrow the possibilities and under "G" I find Gotter. (*Begins to read*) "Age, forty to forty-five. About six feet. One hundred seventy pounds. Birthplace unknown to us. Original occupation unknown to us, although he seems to know Munich and Dresden. Schooling unknown to us. Family unknown to us. No known political connections. No known trade-union connections. Many descriptions, few of them in agreement and none of them of great reliability. Equally unreliable, though often asked for, were Paris, Copenhagen, Brussels police descriptions. Only points on which there is agreement: married to a foreign woman, either American or English; three children; has used name of Gotter, Thomas Bodmer, Karl Francis. Thought to have left Germany in 1933, and to have joined Max Freidank shortly after. Worked closely with Freidank, perhaps directly under his orders. Known to have crossed border in 1934—February, May, June, October. Known to have again crossed border with Max Freidank in 1935—August, twice in October, November, January—"

KURT

(Smiles)

The report is unreliable. It would have been impossible for God to have crossed the border that often.

TECK

(Looks up, laughs. Then looks back at list)

"In 1934, outlaw radio station announcing itself as Radio European, begins to be heard. Station was located in Düsseldorf: the house of a restaurant waiter was searched, and nothing was found. Radio heard during most of 1934 and 1935. In an attempt to locate it, two probable Communists killed in the tool-house of a farm near Bonn. In three of the broadcasts, Gotter known to have crossed border immediately before and after. Radio again became active in early part of 1936. Active attempt made to locate Freidank. Gotter believed to have then appeared in Spain with Madrid Government army, in one of the German brigades, and to have been a brigade commander under previously used name of Bodmer. Known to have stayed in France the first months of 1938.

Again crossed German border some time during week when Hitler's Hamburg radio speech interrupted and went off the air." (*Looks up*) That was a daring deed, Herr Müller. It caused a great scandal. I remember. It amused me.

KURT

It was not done for that reason.

TECK

"Early in 1939, informer in Konstanz reported Gotter's entry, carrying money which had been exchanged in Paris and Brussels. Following day, home of Konstanz Gestapo chief raided for spy list by two men—" (KURT *turns to look at* FANNY *and* DAVID, *smiles*) My God, Herr Müller, that job took two good men.

SARA

(*Angrily*)

Even you admire them.

TECK

Even I. Now I conclude a week ago that you are Gotter, Karl Francis—

KURT

Please. Do not describe me to myself again.

TECK

And that you will be traveling home—(*Points to brief-case*) —with this. But you seem in no hurry, and so I must wait. Last night when I hear that Freidank has been taken, I guess

that you will now be leaving. Not for California. I will tell
you free of charge, Herr Müller, that they have got no information from Freidank or the others.

KURT

Thank you. But I was sure they would not. I know all three
most well. They will take what will be given them.

TECK

(*Looks down. Softly*)
There is a deep sickness in the German character, Herr
Müller. A pain-love, a death-love—

DAVID

(*Very angrily*)
Oh, for God's sake, spare us *your* moral judgments.

FANNY

(*Very sharply*)
Yes. They are sickening. Get on!

KURT

Fanny and David are Americans and they do not understand our world—as yet. (*Turns to* DAVID *and* FANNY) All
Fascists are not of one mind, one stripe. There are those who
give the orders, those who carry out the orders, those who
watch the orders being carried out. Then there are those
who are half in, half hoping to come in. They are made to
do the dishes and clean the boots. Frequently they come in

high places and wish now only to survive. They came late: some because they did not jump in time, some because they were stupid, some because they were shocked at the crudity of the *German* evil, and preferred their own evils, and some because they were fastidious men. For those last, we may well some day have pity. They are lost men, their spoils are small, their day is gone. (*To* TECK) Yes?

TECK
(*Slowly*)

Yes. You have the understanding heart. It will get in your way some day.

KURT
(*Smiles*)

I will watch it.

TECK

We are both men in trouble, Herr Müller. The world, un-gratefully, seems to like your kind even less than it does mine. (*Leans forward*) Now. Let us do business. You will not get back if Von Seitz knows you are going.

KURT

You are wrong. Instead of crawling a hundred feet an hour in deep night, I will walk across the border with as little trouble as if I were a boy again on a summer walking trip. There are many men they would like to have. I would be allowed to walk directly to them—until they had all the names and all the addresses. (*Laughs, points his finger at*

TECK) *Roumanians* would pick me up ahead of time. *Germans* would not.

TECK
(Smiles)

Still the national pride?

KURT

Why not? For that which is good.

FANNY
(Comes over, very angrily, to TECK)

I have not often in my life felt what I feel now. Whatever you are, and however you became it, the picture of a man selling the lives of other men—

TECK

Is very ugly, Madame Fanny. I do not do it without some shame, and therefore I must sink my shame in large money. *(Puts his hand on the brief-case)* The money is here. For ten thousand, you go back to save your friends, nobody will know that you go, and I will give you my good wishes. *(Slowly, deliberately, KURT begins to shake his head. TECK waits, then carefully)* What?

KURT

This money is going home with me. It was not given to me to save my life, and I shall not so use it. It is to save the lives and further the work of more than I. It is important to me to carry on that work and to save the lives of three valuable men, and to do that with all speed. But— (*Sharply*) Count de Brancovis, the first morning we arrived in this house, my children wanted their breakfast with great haste. That is because the evening before we had been able only to buy milk and buns for them. If I would not touch this money for them, I would not touch it for you. (*Very sharply*) It goes back with me. The way it is. And if it does not get back, it is because I will not get back.

(*There is a long pause.* SARA *gets up, turns away.*)

TECK

Then I do not think you will get back. You are a brave one, Herr Müller, but you will not get back.

KURT
(*As if he were very tired*)

I will send to you a postal card and tell you about my bravery.

DAVID
(*Coming toward* KURT)

Is it true that if this swine talks, you and the others will be—

SARA
(*Very softly*)

Caught and killed. Of course. If they're lucky enough to get killed quickly. (*Quietly, points to the table*) You should have seen those hands in 1935.

FANNY

(*Violently, to* DAVID)

We'll give him the money. For God's sake, let's give it to him and get him out of here.

DAVID

(*To* SARA)

Do you want him to go back?

SARA

Yes. I do.

DAVID

All right. (*Goes to her, lifts her face*) You're a good girl.

KURT

That is true. Brave and good, my Sara. She is everything. She is handsome and gay and— (*Puts his hand over his eyes.* SARA *turns away.*)

DAVID

(*After a second, comes to stand near* TECK)

If we give you the money, what is to keep you from selling to Von Seitz?

TECK

I do not like your thinking I would do that. But—

DAVID

(*Tensely*)

Look here. I'm sick of what you'd like or wouldn't like.

146

And I'm sick of your talk. We'll get this over with now, without any more fancy talk from you, or as far as I am concerned, you can get out of here without my money and sell to any buyer you can find. I can't take much more of you at any cost.

TECK

(*Smiles*)

It is your anger which delays us. I was about to say that I understood your fear that I would go to Von Seitz, and I would suggest that you give me a small amount of cash now and a check dated a month from now. In a month, Herr Müller should be nearing home, and he can let you know. And if you should not honor the check because Herr Müller is already in Germany, Von Seitz will pay a little something for a reliable description. I will take my chance on that. You will now say that I could do that in any case—and that is the chance you will take.

DAVID

(*Looks at* KURT, *who does not look up*)

Is a month enough? For you to get back?

KURT

(*Shrugs*)

I do not know.

DAVID

(*To* TECK)

Two months from today. How do you want the cash and how do you want the check?

147

TECK

One month from today. That I will not discuss. One month. Please decide now.

DAVID

(*Sharply*)

All right. (*To* TECK) How do you want it?

TECK

Seventy-five hundred dollars in a check. Twenty-five hundred in cash.

DAVID

I haven't anywhere near that much cash in the house. Leave your address and I'll send it to you in the morning.

TECK

(*Laughs*)

Address? I have no address, and I wish it now. Madame Fanny has cash in her sitting-room safe.

FANNY

Have you investigated that, too?

TECK

(*Laughs*)

No. You once told me you always kept money in the house.

DAVID

(*To* FANNY)

How much have you got upstairs?

FANNY

I don't know. About fifteen or sixteen hundred.

TECK

Very well. That will do. Make the rest in the check.

DAVID

Get it, Mama, please. (*He starts toward the library door.* FANNY *starts for the hall exit.*)

FANNY

(*Turns, looks carefully at* TECK)

Years ago, I heard somebody say that being Roumanian was not a nationality, but a profession. The years have brought no change.

KURT

(*Softly*)

Being a Roumanian aristocrat is a profession.

(FANNY *exits. After her exit, there is silence.* KURT *does not look up,* SARA *does not move.*)

TECK

(*Awkwardly*)

The new world has left the room. (*Looks up at them*) I feel less discomfort with you. We are Europeans, born to trouble and understanding it.

KURT

My wife is not a European.

TECK

Almost. (*Points upstairs*) They are young. The world has gone well for most of them. For us— (*Smiles*) The three of us—we are like peasants watching the big frost. Work, trouble, ruin— (*Shrugs*) But no need to call curses at the frost. There it is, it will be again, always—for us.

SARA

(*Gets up, moves to the window, looks out*)

You mean my husband and I do not have angry words for you. What for? We know how many there are of you. They don't, yet. My mother and brother feel shocked that you are in their house. For us—we have seen you in so many houses.

TECK

I do not say you *want* to understand me, Mrs. Müller. I say only that you do.

SARA

Yes. You are not difficult to understand.

KURT

(*Slowly gets up, stands stiffly. Then he moves toward the decanter table*)

A whiskey?

TECK

No, thank you. (*He turns his head to watch* KURT *move.*
He turns back.)

KURT

Sherry?

TECK
(*Nods*)

Thank you, I will.

KURT
(*As he pours*)

You, too, wish to go back to Europe.

TECK

Yes.

KURT

But they do not much want you. Not since the Budapest
oil deal of '31.

TECK

You seem as well informed about me as I am about you.

KURT

That must have been a conference of high comedy, that
one. Everybody trying to guess whether Kessler was working
for Fritz Thyssen, and what Thyssen *really* wanted—and
whether this "National Socialism" was a smart blind of
Thyssen's, and where was Wolff—I should like to have seen

you and your friends. It is too bad: you guessed an inch off, eh?

TECK

More than an inch.

KURT

And Kessler has a memory? (*Almost playfully*) I do not think Von Seitz would pay you money for a description of a man who has a month to travel. But I think he would pay you in a visa and a cable to Kessler. I think you want a visa almost as much as you want money. Therefore, I conclude you will try for the money here, and the visa from Von Seitz. (*He comes toward the table carrying the sherry glass*) I cannot get anywhere near Germany in a month and you know it. (*He is about to place the glass on the table*) I have been bored with this talk of paying you money. If they are willing to try you on this fantasy, I am not. Whatever made you think I would take such a chance? Or *any* chance? You're a gambler. But you should not gamble with your life. (TECK *has turned to stare at him, made a half motion as if to rise. As he does so, and on the words, "gamble with your life," * KURT *drops the glass, hits* TECK *in the face. Struggling,* TECK *makes a violent effort to rise.* KURT *throws himself on* TECK, *knocking him to the floor. As* TECK *falls to the floor,* KURT *hits him on the side of the head. At the fourth blow,* TECK *does not move.* KURT *rises, takes the gun from his pocket, begins to lift* TECK *from the floor. As he does so,* JOSHUA *appears in the hall entrance. He is washed and ready for dinner. As he reaches the door, he stops, sees the scene, stands quietly as if he were waiting for orders.* KURT *begins to balance* TECK,

152

to balance himself. To JOSHUA) Hilf mir. (JOSHUA *comes quickly to* KURT) Mach die Tür auf! (JOSHUA *runs toward the doors, opens them, stands waiting*) Bleib da! Mach die Tür zu! (KURT *begins to move out through the terrace. When he is outside the doors,* JOSHUA *closes them quickly, stands looking at his mother.*)

SARA

There's trouble.

JOSHUA

Do not worry. I will go up now. I will pack. In ten minutes all will be ready. I will say nothing. I will get the children ready— (*He starts quickly for the hall, turns for a second to look toward the terrace doors. Then almost with a sob*) This was a nice house.

SARA

(*Softly*)

We're not going this time, darling. There's no need to pack.

JOSHUA

(*Stares at her, puzzled*)

But Papa—

SARA

Go upstairs, Joshua. Take Babbie and Bodo in your room, and close the door. Stay there until I call you. (*He looks at her,* SARA *sits down*) There's nothing to be frightened of, darling. Papa is all right. (*Then very softly*) Papa is going home.

JOSHUA

To Germany?

SARA

Yes.

JOSHUA

Oh. Alone?

SARA

Alone. (*Very softly*) Don't say anything to the children. He will tell them himself.

JOSHUA

I won't.

SARA

(*As he hesitates*)

I'm all right. Go upstairs now. (*He moves slowly out, she watches him, he disappears. For a minute she sits quietly. Then she gets up, moves to the terrace doors, stands with her hands pressed against them. Then she crosses, picks up the overturned chair, places it by the table, picks up the glass, puts it on the table. As if without knowing what she is doing, she wipes the table with her handkerchief.*)

(FANNY *comes in from hall. After a second,* DAVID *comes in from library. Stops, looks around room.*)

DAVID

Where is he? Upstairs?

SARA

No. They went outside.

FANNY

Outside? They went outside. What are they doing, picking a bouquet together?

SARA

(*Without turning*)

They just went outside.

DAVID

(*Looks at her*)

What's the matter, Sara?

(SARA *shakes her head. Goes to the desk, opens the telephone book, looks at a number, begins to dial the telephone.*)

FANNY

Eleven hundred, eleven hundred and fifty, twelve, twelve-fifty—

DAVID

For God's sake, stop counting that money.

FANNY

All right. I'm nervous. And I don't like to think of giving him too much.

SARA

It's very nice of you and Mama. All that money— (*Into*

155

the telephone) Hello. What time is your next plane? Oh.
To— South. To El Paso, or—Brownsville. Yes.

DAVID

(*To* FANNY)

Is Joseph ready?

FANNY

I don't know. I told him I'd call him.

SARA

To Brownsville? Yes. Yes. That's all right. At what time?
Yes. No. The ticket will be picked up at the airport. (DAVID
begins to cross to the bell cord. She looks up) No. David.
Don't call Joseph. *David! Please!* (*He draws back, stares at
her. Looking at him, she goes on with the conversation*)
Ritter. R-I-T-T-E-R. From Chicago. Yes. Yes. (*She hangs
up, walks away.*)

DAVID

Sara! What's happening? What is all this? (*She does not
answer*) Where is Kurt? What— (*He starts for the terrace
door.*)

SARA

David. *Don't go out.*

FANNY

(*Rises*)

Sara! What's happening—

SARA

For seven years now, day in, day out, men have crossed

the German border. They are always in danger. They always may be going in to die. Did you ever see the face of a man who never knows if this day will be the last day? (*Softly*) Don't go out on the terrace, David. Leave Kurt alone.

FANNY
(*Softly*)

Sara! What is—

SARA
(*Quietly*)

For them, it may be torture, and it may be death. Some day, when it's all over, maybe there'll be a few of them left to celebrate. There aren't many of Kurt's age left. He couldn't take a chance on them. They wouldn't have liked it. (*Suddenly, violently*) He'd have had a bad time trying to explain to them that because of this house and this nice town and my mother and my brother, he took chances with their work and with their lives. (*Quietly*) Sit down, Mama. I think it's all over now. (*To* DAVID) There's nothing you can do about it. It's the way it had to be.

DAVID

Sara—

FANNY

Do you mean what I think you— (*Sinks slowly into her chair.*)

SARA

(*She turns, looks out toward the doors. After a pause*) He's going away tonight and he's never coming back any more. (*In a sing-song*) Never, never, never. (*She looks down at her hands, as if she were very interested in them*) I don't like to be alone at night. I guess everybody in the world's got a time in the day they don't like. Me, it's right before I go to sleep. And now it's going to be for always. All the rest of my life. (*She looks up as* KURT *comes in from the terrace*) I've told them. There is an eight-thirty plane going as far south as Brownsville. I've made you a reservation. In the name of Ritter.

KURT

(*Stands looking at her*)

Liebe Sara! (*Then he goes to the table at which* FANNY *is sitting. To* FANNY) It is hard for you, eh? (*He pats her hand*) I am sorry.

FANNY

(*Without knowing why, she takes her hand away*)

Hard? I don't know. I— I don't— I don't know what I want to say.

KURT

(*Looks at the hand she has touched, then turns to look at* DAVID)

Before I come in, I stand and think. I say, I will make Fanny and David understand. I say, how can I? Does one understand a killing? No. To hell with it, I say. I do what must be done. I have long sickened of words when I see the men who live by them. What do you wish to make them understand, I ask myself. Wait. Stand here. Just stand here. What are you thinking? Say it to them just as it comes to you. And this is what came to me. When you kill in a war, it is not so lonely; and I remember a cousin I have not seen for many years; and a melody comes back and I begin to make it with my fingers; a staircase in a house in Bonn years ago; an old dog who used to live in our town; Sara in a hundred places— Shame on us. Thousands of years and we cannot yet make a world. Like a child I am. I have stopped a man's life. (*Points to the place on the couch where he had been sitting opposite* TECK) I sit here. I listen to him. You will not believe—but I pray that I will not have to touch him. Then I know I will have to. I know that if I do not, it is only that I pamper myself, and risk the lives of others. I want you from the room. I know what I must do. (*Loudly*) All right. Do I now pretend sorrow? Do I now pretend it is not I who act thus? No. I do it. I have done it. I will do it again. And I will keep my hope that we may make a world in which all men can die in bed. I have a great hate for the violent. They are the sick of the world. (*Softly*) Maybe I am sick now, too.

SARA

You aren't sick. Stop that. It's late. You must go soon.

KURT

(*Looks up at her*)

Maybe all that I have ever wanted is a land that would let me have you. (*Then without looking away from her, he puts out his hands, she touches them*) I am going to say good-bye now to my children. Then I am going to take your car— (*Motions with his head*) I will take him with me. After that, it is up to you. Two ways: You can let me go and keep silent.

I believe I can hide him and the car. At the end of two days, if they have not been found, you will tell as much of the truth as is safe for you to say. Tell them the last time you saw us we were on our way to Washington. You did not worry at the absence, we might have rested there. Two crazy foreigners fight, one gets killed, you know nothing of the reason. I will have left the gun, there will be no doubt who did the killing. If you will give me those two days, I think I will be far enough away from here. If the car is found before then— (*Shrugs*) I will still try to move with speed. And all that will make you, for yourselves, part of a murder. For the world, I do not think you will be in bad trouble. (*He pauses*) There is another way. You can call your police. You can tell them the truth. I will not get home. (*To* SARA) I wish to see the children now.

(*She goes out into the hall and up the stairs. There is silence.*)

FANNY

What are you thinking, David?

DAVID

I don't know. What are you thinking?

FANNY

Me? Oh, I was thinking about my Joshua. I was thinking that a few months before he died, we were sitting out there. (*Points to terrace*) He said, "Fanny, the Renaissance American is dying, the Renaissance man is dying." I said what do you mean, although I knew what he meant, I always knew. "A Renaissance man," he said, "is a man who wants to know. He wants to know how fast a bird will fly, how thick is the crust of the earth, what made Iago evil, how to plow a field. He knows there is no dignity to a mountain, if there is no dignity to man. You can't put that in a man, but when it's *really* there, and he will fight for it, put your trust in him."

DAVID

(Gets up, smiles, looks at FANNY)

You're a smart woman sometimes. (SARA *enters with* JOSHUA. *To* KURT) Don't worry about things here. My soul doesn't have to be so nice and clean. I'll take care of it. You'll have your two days. And good luck to you.

FANNY

You go with my blessing, too. I like you.

(BODO *enters.*)

SARA

See? I come from good stock.

(KURT *looks at* DAVID. *Then he begins to smile. Nods to* DAVID. *Turns, smiles at* FANNY.)

FANNY

Do you like me?

KURT

I like you, Madame, very much.

FANNY

Would you be able to cash that check?

KURT
(*Laughs*)

Oh, no.

FANNY

Then take the cash. I, too, would like to contribute to your work.

KURT
(*Slowly*)

All right. Thank you. (*He takes the money from the table, puts it in his pocket.*)

BODO
(*To* KURT)

You like Grandma? I thought you would, with time. I like her, too. Sometimes she dilates with screaming, but— Dilates is correct?

(BABETTE *enters.* JOSHUA *stands away from the others, looking at his father.* KURT *turns to look at him.*)

JOSHUA

Alles in Ordnung?

KURT

Alles in Ordnung.

BODO

What? What does that mean, all is well?

(*There is an awkward silence.*)

BABETTE
(*As if she sensed it*)

We are all clean for dinner. But nobody else is clean. And I have on Grandma's dress to me—

FANNY
(*Very nervously*)

Of course. And you look very pretty. You're a pretty little girl, Babbie.

BODO
(*Looks around the room*)

What is the matter? Everybody is acting like such a ninny. I got that word from Grandma.

KURT

Come here. (*They look at him. Then slowly* BABETTE *comes toward him, followed by* BODO. JOSHUA *comes more slowly, to stand at the side of* KURT's *chair*) We have said many good-byes to each other, eh? We must now say another. (*As they stare at him, he smiles, slowly, as if it were difficult*) This time, I leave you with good people to whom I believe you also will be good. (*Half playfully*) Would you allow me to give away my share in you, until I come back?

BABETTE
(*Slowly*)

If you would like it.

KURT

Good. To your mother, her share. My share, to Fanny and David. It is all and it is the most I have to give. (*Laughs*) There. I have made a will, eh? Now. We will not joke. I have something to say to you. It is important for me to say it.

JOSHUA
(*Softly*)

You are talking to us as if we were children.

KURT
(*Turns to look at him*)

Am I, Joshua? I wish you were children. I wish I could say love your mother, do not eat too many sweets, clean your teeth— (*Draws* BODO *to him*) I cannot say these things. You are not children. I took it all away from you.

BABETTE

We have had a most enjoyable life, Papa.

KURT
(*Smiles*)

You are a gallant little liar. And I thank you for it. I have done something bad today—

164

FANNY
(Shocked, sharply)

Kurt—

SARA

Don't, Mama.

(BODO *and* BABETTE *have looked at* FANNY *and* SARA, *puzzled. Then they have turned again to look at* KURT.)

KURT

It is not to frighten you. In a few days, your mother and David will tell you.

BODO

You could not do a bad thing.

BABETTE
(Proudly)

You could not.

KURT
(Shakes his head)

Now let us get straight together. The four of us. Do you remember when we read about "Les Misérables"? Do you remember that we talked about it afterwards and Bodo got candy on Mama's bed?

BODO

I remember.

KURT

Well. He stole bread. The world is out of shape we said,

when there are hungry men. And until it gets in shape, men will steal and lie and—(*A little more slowly*)—kill. But for whatever reason it is done, and whoever does it—you understand me—it is all bad. I want you to remember that. Whoever does it, it is bad. (*Then very gaily*) But you will live to see the day when it will not have to be. All over the world, in every place and every town, there are men who are going to make sure it will not have to be. They want what I want: a childhood for every child. For my children, and I for theirs. (*He picks* BODO *up, rises*) Think of that. It will make you happy. In every town and every village and every mud hut in the world, there is always a man who loves children and who will fight to make a good world for them. And now good-bye. Wait for me. I shall try to come back for you. (*He moves toward the hall, followed by* BABETTE, *and more slowly, by* JOSHUA) Or you shall come to me. At Hamburg, the boat will come in. It will be a fine, safe land— I will be waiting on the dock. And there will be the three of you and Mama and Fanny and David. And I will have ordered an extra big dinner and we will show them what our Germany can be like— (*He has put* BODO *down. He leans down, presses his face in* BABETTE'S *hair. Tenderly, as her mother has done earlier, she touches his hair.*)

JOSHUA

Of course. That is the way it will be. Of course. But— but if you should find yourself delayed— (*Very slowly*) Then I will come to you. Mama.

SARA

(*She has turned away*)

I heard you, Joshua.

KURT

(*He kisses* BABETTE)

Gute Nacht, Liebling!

BABETTE

Gute Nacht, Papa. Mach's gut!

KURT

(*Leans to kiss* BODO)

Good night, baby.

BODO

Good night, Papa. Mach's gut!

(BABETTE *runs up the steps. Slowly* BODO *follows her.*)

KURT

(*Kisses* JOSHUA)

Good night, son.

JOSHUA

Good night, Papa. Mach's gut! (*He begins to climb the steps.* KURT *stands watching them, smiling. When they disappear, he turns to* DAVID.)

KURT

Good-bye, and thank you.

DAVID

Good-bye, and good luck.

KURT

(*He moves to* FANNY)

Good-bye. I have good children, eh?

FANNY

Yes, you have. (KURT *kisses her hand.*)

KURT

(*Slowly, he turns toward* SARA)

Men who wish to live have the best chance to live. I wish to live. I wish to live with you. (*She comes toward him.*)

SARA

For twenty years. It is as much for me today— (*Takes his arms*) Just once, and for all my life. (*He pulls her toward him*) Come back for me, darling. If you can. (*Takes brief-case from table and gives it to him.*)

KURT

(*Simply*)

I will try. (*He turns*) Good-bye, to you all. (*He exits. After a second, there is the sound of a car starting. They sit listening to it. Gradually the noise begins to go off into the distance. A second later,* JOSHUA *appears.*)